Gilles Villeneuve

A photographic portrait

Joseph Gilles Henri Villeneuve was born on 18 January 1950 in St Jean sur Richelieu, Québec, Canada. He married Joann Barthe in 1970, and they had two children, Jacques in 1971 and Melanie in 1973. His hobbies included photography and playing the piano, and watching downhill skiing and ice skating. He liked to listen to The Beatles and The Animals, and his favourite films were 'Bullitt', 'Convoy', and 'Smokey and the Bandit'. He died on 8 May 1982 in Louvain, Belgium.

© Quentin Spurring (photo commentary)
and Nigel Roebuck (introduction), 2007

First published in June 2007

A catalogue record for this book is available from the British Library

ISBN 978 1 84425 630 3

Library of Congress control no 2007922004

Published by Haynes Publishing,
Sparkford, Yeovil, Somerset BA22 7JJ, UK
Tel: 01963 442030 Fax: 01963 440001
Int. tel: +44 1963 442030 Int. fax: +44 1963 440001
E-mail: sales@haynes.co.uk
Website: www.haynes.co.uk

Haynes North America Inc.
861 Lawrence Drive, Newbury Park,
California 91320, USA

All pictures in this book are courtesy of LAT Photographic, with the exception of pages 18-19 (Gilles-Villeneuve Museum Collection, www.gilles.villeneuve.com) and page 111 (Martin Holmes).

The publisher wishes to thank all at LAT for their collaboration on this book, and in particular Peter Higham, Kathy Ager, Tim Wright, Kevin Wood, Stephen Carpenter, Matt Smith and Emma Champion.

Design and layout by Richard Parsons

Printed and bound in Great Britain by
J. H. Haynes & Co. Ltd

CONTENTS PAGE Gilles concentrates hard in the uncompetitive Ferrari 312T5 during the 1980 Belgian Grand Prix at Zolder, where he finished sixth.

Gilles Villeneuve

A photographic portrait

Photographs by **LAT** • Photo commentary by **Quentin Spurring** • Reminiscences by **Nigel Roebuck**

CONTENTS

Introduction   6

1967–1974
THE MULTIPLE SNOWMOBILE CHAMPION   18

1975–1976
A SPRINGBOARD TO FAME IN ATLANTIC   20

1977
F1 DEBUTS FOR McLAREN AND FERRARI   28

1978
A DREAM COMES TRUE IN MONTREAL   52

1979
A TRIPLE WINNER IN A FERRARI 1–2   70

1980
TRAPPED IN AN UNCOMPETITIVE CAR   118

1981
TWO GREAT VICTORIES WITH THE TURBO   140

1982
A CHAMPIONSHIP BID CUT SHORT   182

Race Results   206

Gilles Villeneuve

BY NIGEL ROEBUCK

OPPOSITE Gilles is clearly a happy man as he prepares to make his Formula 1 debut for McLaren in the 1977 British Grand Prix at Silverstone. He was already 27 years old, and had previously contested 44 car races, winning 19 of them. Gilles was looking forward to his maiden race here and several more with McLaren later in the season, but it was not to be.

"Look at him," said Jacques Laffite. "He's different from the rest of us – on a separate level."

It is not often that a Grand Prix driver says that about another, but it was a fact that Gilles Villeneuve could do things with a racing car beyond the scope of anyone else. This particular day – October 5 1979 – conditions were foul at Watkins Glen, and the track was awash when the session began. Not many drivers went out, and those who did were swiftly back in again. Fastest, by some way, was the Ferrari of newly crowned World Champion Jody Scheckter.

Then we saw a Ferrari mechanic carrying a small figure across the river in pit lane, and Laffite, snug in his Elf jacket, had to let everyone know. "Gilles!" he cried. "He's going out!" Away the Ferrari rumbled, and then instant sky-high revs had everyone giggling nervously: Gilles was never much of one for 'exploratory' laps.

When it skittered by the first time, the T4 was moving at a speed we hadn't seen before, and every lap seemed more extravagant, more on the edge. You could call it foolhardy, and some did, but none could deny the artistry or the courage. Laffite savoured what he was seeing, marvelling that it was possible.

In came Villeneuve finally, steam curling from the hot Michelins. He'd loved it, being out there in those conditions, just as he would relish flying his helicopter at low level in fog: "Every nerve end is alive..."

Gilles had lapped almost 11 seconds faster than Jody. *Eleven seconds*. Two days later, by almost a minute, Villeneuve won the US Grand Prix.

Years later Laffite reflected on that day at the Glen. "No human being can do a miracle, you know, but Gilles made you wonder..."

Looking back on Gilles Villeneuve, it is easy to be swayed by mythology, to remember him as the perfect racing driver, the man without flaw. He was neither, of course, but undeniably he was a special force in this sport, with genius and charisma to throw away. When he died, at Zolder in May 1982, a flame was snuffed out in motor racing which, for many, has never been properly rekindled.

It was a short career – just four full seasons – in Formula 1, and his 67 Grands Prix yielded but six wins. If dry statistics are your bible, Villeneuve will not trouble you – any more than will Jochen Rindt, another who won only half a dozen times. But if you saw either man race, numbers will not concern you. You saw grandeur on the race track, that much you know.

I think of the Saturday at Dijon in 1981. This was a place Villeneuve enjoyed, the circuit at which he and René Arnoux had fought their mesmeric battle two years earlier. Then, though, Gilles had been in the Ferrari T4, a much wieldier car than the turbocharged 126C he was driving now.

In point of fact, he had mixed feelings about the 126C. On the one hand, it was mighty heavy, and had, in Harvey Postlethwaite's estimation, "About one quarter of the downforce of a Williams or Brabham". On the other, it had a lot of horsepower, and, according to Gilles, a surprisingly benign nature: "It's like a big red Cadillac," he said. "You can get it *unbelievably* sideways – and it comes back..."

So there we were at Dijon, watching at the Courbe de Pouas, a long, undulating, right-hander, with no run-off worth the name. In the morning he had crashed there, and during the lunch break I found him dabbing a cut on his jaw. "Bloody catch fence pole cracked my helmet and broke the visor..."

"You overdid it?" I asked. "Just ran out of road?" "No, no," Gilles grinned. "I ran out of *lock!* The car is really bad

through there – go and have a look this afternoon."

I did. I watched the Williams and Brabhams drone through on their rails, and waited.

At its clipping point, at the top of a rise, the Ferrari was already sideways. As it came past me, plunging downhill now, the tail stayed out of line, and *still* Gilles had his foot hard down. As it reached the bottom of the dip, it was virtually broadside, Villeneuve's head pointing up the road – out of the side of the cockpit.

Somehow, though, the car did not spin, finally snapping back into line as it grazed the catch fencing, then rocketing away up the hill. Charles Cevert, brother of the late François, whooped with delight, and David Hobbs looked aghast. "That's genius," he said. "Are you seriously telling me he's won two Grands Prix in *that?*"

Through that season a couple of French doctors were engaged in research into the strains imposed on a man by driving a Formula 1 car, and all that day Villeneuve was 'wired up', his heartbeat monitored. During the morning session, prior to his accident, his rate never exceeded 127, and when he hit the fence there was a flash reading of 168.

These were extraordinarily low figures – particularly when compared with those of Gilles's team mate, Didier Pironi, whose heart thumped away at 170-207 throughout the Monaco Grand Prix.

As I read the doctors' report, I remembered a 'phone conversation with Chris Amon in the summer of 1977, during which Gilles drove Chris's CanAm Wolf. "In all my years in racing," Amon said, "I've never seen anyone behave like he does after a shunt. I mean, he doesn't react at all..."

"Is he quick?" I asked, the most time-honoured question in motor racing. *"Quick?"* Amon retorted. "Jesus, he might be quicker than anyone I've ever seen!"

It was after the Formula Atlantic race at Trois-Rivières in 1976 that we in Europe first began to take serious notice of Villeneuve. Back then it was the custom to invite a few Formula 1 drivers to take part in the series' blue riband event: the money was good, and James Hunt went over, along with Alan Jones and the Patricks, Depailler and Tambay.

When Hunt got back, Villeneuve was all he could talk about. "You only needed to watch him for a couple of minutes to know," said James. "We were driving identical cars for the same team. In Formula 1 I reckoned I was as quick as anyone at that time, and I couldn't get near him. I told Marlboro and McLaren to sign him as soon as possible."

A few days later Teddy Mayer had a contract drawn up. The deal was that Gilles would drive a third car in four or five Grands Prix in 1977, with McLaren taking an option on him for '78. The money on offer was good – *very* good, given that ultimately he drove only one race for McLaren, at Silverstone.

In those days Formula 1 was over-subscribed, and no fewer than 14 drivers took part in pre-qualifying, with the fastest four eligible for qualifying proper.

Amon's endorsement of Villeneuve was fresh in my mind when I arrived at Silverstone, and immediately had my first sight of Gilles's McLaren M23, at Copse. It was travelling backwards.

"You had a lot of spins today," I said later. "Yes," Gilles replied. "I've had no chance to test, and this is the fastest car I've ever driven, and the fastest track I've ever seen. I had to learn both in a short time, and the quickest way to find the limit is to go over it..."

Gilles went on to qualify ninth, faster than regular McLaren driver Jochen Mass, in the new M26. Faster, too, than the Ferrari of Carlos Reutemann.

In the race Gilles ran seventh – ahead of Mass – then saw that his water temperature was rising. In he came, losing two laps before the mechanics discovered that the gauge was faulty. Rejoining immediately behind the leaders, in the ensuing laps he lost very little to them. At the end he was 11th, Mass fourth. Do the math, as they say.

Already Villeneuve's fighting spirit had made an indelible impression. In time it was something we took for granted, but then we marvelled at the way he charged on, setting the fifth fastest lap. Watching TV in the farmhouse at Fiorano, Enzo Ferrari was much intrigued.

Now Villeneuve had sampled Formula 1, and was chastened when Teddy Mayer said he was not intending to exercise McLaren's option on him for 1978.

"That put me down a bit, because I couldn't understand why – I thought I'd gone well at Silverstone. At first I thought, no problem, I'll find a place in another team, but time was going by, and nothing was happening. Then, out of nowhere, I got a call from Ferrari, asking if I would like to drive for them! I took the next flight to Italy..."

Thus began the saga of Gilles Villeneuve and Ferrari, for whom he would drive for the rest of his life. In 1978

OPPOSITE In the cockpit of the Ferrari 312T4 prior to the 1979 British Grand Prix at Silverstone that followed his sensational performance at Dijon. Gilles was now a three-times Grand Prix winner and this was his best season in a 3-litre Ferrari. The stylised 'V' on either side of his black and red helmet was devised by his wife, Joann.

James Hunt on Gilles, Trois Rivières, 1976: "You only needed to watch him for a couple of minutes to know. We were driving identical cars for the same team. In Formula 1 I reckoned I was as quick as anyone at that time, and I couldn't get near him. I told Marlboro and McLaren to sign him as soon as possible."

OPPOSITE A little
wide-eyed after
emerging from a
substantial wreck in the
1980 season-opening
Argentine Grand Prix.
Gilles had the dreadful
Ferrari 312T5 in a
very unlikely second
place when something
broke in the front
suspension. He was a
helpless passenger as
the car ploughed off
the circuit, through the
catchfencing and hard
into the barrier.

he partnered Reutemann, and by Long Beach, race four, was confident enough to lead for 40 laps before tangling with Clay Regazzoni, who was being lapped.

At the next race, Monaco, there was another accident, this time when his left front tyre went down in the tunnel. The Ferrari clouted a guardrail, then hurtled out into the sunlight on three wheels. In the paddock I was amazed by Gilles's *sang-froid*. Had he no sense of fear, or what?

"I don't have any fear of a crash," he said at once. "Of course, in a top-gear corner I don't want to crash – I'm not crazy. But if it's near the end of qualifying, maybe, then I guess you can squeeze the fear...

"I never hurt myself at all until I broke my leg in an Atlantic race in '74, and that was interesting, because I hit a guardrail, and I'd always been scared of that. Afterwards I wasn't worried any more, because now I knew what it was like: you hurt yourself, and they mend you, and that's it."

The Monaco accident, though, had been at very high speed. Had it not frightened him at all? "Me, no. The car, yes. I thought, 'Bloody hell, I'm going to have a nice one here!' I never think I can hurt myself – it seems impossible to me – but I know I can hurt the car, and that's what I don't want to do."

Patrick Tambay: "Everything in Gilles's life was done at 200mph – skiing, driving his speedboat, whatever. In the winter we'd sometimes play Monopoly, and even then it was like he was driving his Formula 1 car – very decisive, never hesitating, taking risks, going forward all the time."

Even in 1978, that came across as a radical philosophy, but it was Villeneuve true, and it never changed. As I came to realise over the years, he was like that in everything.

"Everything in Gilles's life," said Patrick Tambay, "was done at 200mph – skiing, driving his speedboat, whatever. In the winter we'd sometimes play Monopoly, and even then it was like he was driving his Formula 1 car – very decisive, never hesitating, taking risks, going forward all the time. Once his mind was made up, he'd go for it."

He went for it, too, in what he said. Even then it was a brave man who would criticise the powers-that-be, whether the FIA or Bernie Ecclestone, but Gilles never held back: "But it's the *truth*, isn't it?"

Over time, as he grew more confident in his environment, his language became saltier, his sense of humour ever sharper, not least about his brother, then competing in Atlantic. What was this, I said once, about Jacques jumping the start last weekend?

"I was right there on the start line, and when he'd moved a few feet I said, 'Jesus, he has a good start!' Nobody else had moved yet. Then he had done 50 metres – and *still* nobody had moved! I thought, 'Whoaaa, something wrong there'. He'd gone on the red light! He jumped the start by eight seconds...what do you do? So he reverses back towards the grid – and then they gave signal to start! They were going one way, and he was coming the other. I think," Gilles said thoughtfully, "there should be some way of stopping everything when that happens, because it's fucking dangerous if you get the green light, and someone's backing up towards you..."

Made sense to me.

Through 1978 nothing could live with the Lotus 79, but Ferrari's T3 sometimes offered decent opposition to Mario Andretti and Ronnie Peterson. At Monza Villeneuve qualified second to Andretti, and led him away, but behind them there was carnage, an accident involving 10 cars, one of them the Lotus of Peterson.

When the surviving cars came to a halt at the end of the lap, the drivers climbed out, shocked, but Villeneuve remained in his car, not even removing his helmet.

"After the race was stopped," he said, "I didn't want to get involved. Obviously, there was going to be a restart eventually, and I didn't want to know at that stage who was hurt or maybe dead. I looked at the drivers, obviously agitated, and I didn't think that was a good frame of mind to be in, so I stayed clear of it."

After an hour, the race was restarted, and Villeneuve was away like a shot, Andretti going with him. "Gilles had really matured," said Mario. "He drove to the limit of the car, but he made no mistakes. And I knew when I tried to go by him, he was going to give me some race track."

Eventually, inevitably, the Lotus did get by the Ferrari, but both were penalised a minute for jumping the start, and put back to sixth and seventh. "I was pissed off," Gilles said, "until I heard about Ronnie..." Peterson died during the night.

More than once during this, his first full season, Villeneuve had threatened to win a Grand Prix, but when it happened, in Montréal, he had mixed feelings, for it hadn't come quite the way he would have wished. Only when the Lotus of Jean-Pierre Jarier retired did he take the lead.

Later Gilles told me he could remember little of it. "It might sound crazy, but I felt kind of embarrassed. OK, I'd driven flat out, but the win meant less because I felt I'd inherited it. Everyone was slapping me on the back, but somehow I didn't feel part of it. On the podium, Pierre Trudeau (then the Canadian Prime Minister) was waving a Ferrari flag, and it seemed unreal this was all for me."

If Gilles won that inaugural race on the Isle Notre-

Dame, it is his drive the following year that lives in the mind. Jody Scheckter, now his Ferrari team mate, won the World Championship in 1979, but by this time Jody had one eye on retirement, and collected most of his points by stealth.

"It seemed to me," said James Hunt, "that Villeneuve did everything possible *not* to win the title that year. He had massive natural talent, and was definitely the quickest driver – but surely the main reason anyone goes racing is to win the World Championship, isn't it?"

Not in Villeneuve's case, no. "For me, the thing is to win races," he said, "and if you do that enough, the championship will come along automatically. But cruising sometimes, looking for points...come on! A title won that way would mean nothing. Remember Ronnie Peterson never won it, and then look at some of the guys who did..."

Early in 1979 Gilles had won at Kyalami and Long Beach, but the competitiveness of the Ferrari T4 was not consistent, race to race. Although the flat-12 engine was stronger than a Cosworth DFV, its shape militated against the building of a true 'ground effects' chassis, and the T4 simply didn't have the grip of a Williams or Ligier, or the power of the turbocharged Renault.

Gilles, though, went into every race with the hope – the *intention* – of winning. He took the fight to the Renaults at Dijon, led away at the Osterreichring (from the third row!), battled with Jones's Williams at Zandvoort – but it was Scheckter who kept on quietly banking the points.

By the time of Monza the situation was that if Scheckter won there, the World Championship was his, beyond Villeneuve's reach. On lap 13 they moved into first and second positions, where they remained to the flag, a tenth apart.

Imagine the call on a driver's integrity in that situation. I asked Gilles if he could have passed Jody. "I hoped like hell he'd break!" he grinned. "But I knew the rules of the game. I'd given my word."

The championship settled, there was no need of team orders at Montréal and Watkins Glen, and it was always on the cards that the leading protagonists would be Jones and Villeneuve.

They qualified 1-2 in Canada, and Gilles took an immediate lead. Jones's Williams might be quicker, but that was no reason to run up the white flag. For 50 laps they ran away on their own, and then Jones made his move into the hairpin, leaning the Williams against the Ferrari. It was hard but fair, and typified the way these two would always fight.

"I thought, 'I've done it!'," said Alan, "and once I was into the lead, I built up a bit of a cushion. But as soon as I

backed off a fraction, there was that bloody red shitbox in my mirrors again! Villeneuve was unbelievable like that – I mean, he *never* gave up. I couldn't help feeling a bit sorry for him. It was his home race, and he drove the wheels off that thing.

"I always loved racing against Gilles, because if you'd won the corner, he'd always give you room, and therefore I'd do the same for him. He was the best driver I ever raced against, and I always knew where I was with him. He'd never do a Piquet on you, and edge you into a wall."

Some defeats are more triumphant than victories. On the podium Gilles looked happier than a year earlier, when he had stood on the top step. "Today I had to fight, and that's what I love."

Gilles won the final race of 1979, at the Glen, but it would be a long time before there was a whiff of victory again. In 1980 the Ferrari T5 was outclassed, but if he grew weary of working with loaves and fishes, it never showed in his performance, and the litmus test of a really great driver, surely, is how he behaves in adversity. I think of Monaco, of a drive from 13th to fifth after a tyre stop, of the late laps, when it began to rain, and all were on slicks, and Villeneuve was lapping five seconds faster than anyone else.

At Imola Gilles had a fright, and admitted as much. Early in the race a rear tyre went down before Tosa, and the Ferrari hit the bank, then bounced back onto the track. When I found him after the race, he had such a severe headache that the doctors had ruled out using his helicopter that night. "I could hear all these engines around me," he said, "but I couldn't see – I thought I'd been blinded, and I can't describe the fear I felt. Before today I'd only ever thought about broken bones..."

In qualifying at Imola Villeneuve had tried Ferrari's prototype turbo car, and although the chassis was plainly agricultural, there was no doubt about the horsepower. Gilles looked to 1981 with a degree of cautious optimism, but at the same time was sorry to lose Scheckter as a team mate. As Jody retired, so Pironi arrived.

After a season with the lithe Ligier, Didier was taken aback by Ferrari's idea of a contemporary Grand Prix car, but he was impressed by the turbocharged V6, and revelled in being a Maranello man. Quiet and outwardly shy, Pironi's innate arrogance and ambition were hidden away – for now.

OPPOSITE At Silverstone in 1981 with Mario Andretti, who was enduring a grim experience with Alfa Romeo in his last full Formula 1 season. In 1982, after Gilles's death and Didier Pironi's career-ending injuries at Hockenheim, Mario answered Enzo Ferrari's call to race at Monza alongside Patrick Tambay. Aged 42, he put a 126C2 on pole position.

Alan Jones: "I always loved racing against Gilles, because if you'd won the corner, he'd always give you room, and therefore I'd do the same for him. He was the best driver I ever raced against, and I always knew where I was with him."

In fact, he had little cause to be arrogant in 1981. Once in a while he out-qualified Gilles, but usually was nowhere near him. At Monaco Gilles qualified second, Didier 17th; in the race number 27 won, while 28 was fourth – and lapped.

This was a race the Ferrari 126C should never have won. "I was behind Gilles at first," said Jones. "He was holding me up a bit, and most guys would just sit there, but he was smarter than that. That old tank of his was heavy as hell, and he knew if he stayed ahead of me he soon wasn't going to have any brakes. So he let me by into Mirabeau – and by that I mean he left me a gap about an inch wider than my car! He didn't make it easy, but it was there if I wanted it, and I knew that gap wouldn't close once I was into it.

"Later on I had a problem, and, sure enough, my mirrors were soon full of red! He was on me as we came down the pit straight, and I did what he'd done – left him a narrow gap if he chose to go for it, which of course he did. He won the race, and the greatest compliment I can pay him is to say that, if I had to have a problem, I'm glad he was the one to benefit from it."

"I'm sore everywhere right now," said Villeneuve afterwards. "This is quite a tiring place, anyway, but with the go-kart ride we all have, it was worse than usual. Bang, bang, bang! All the way through my helmet was hitting the roll-over bar. It's crazy the way the cars are now – no suspension movement at all. The beating the cars are taking is incredible."

Villeneuve's consistency around Monaco was remarkable. After 10 laps, his average lap time was 1m 30.94s; after 20, 1-30.74; after 30, 1-30.50; after 40, 1-30.34; after 50, 1-30.30; after 60, 1-30.22; after 70, 1-30.27; at the finish, 1-30.30.

Two weeks later, at Jarama, he did it again. After qualifying only seventh at the tight track, he was up to third by the first corner, passed Reutemann on lap two, and then took the lead when Jones spun.

Now the work began. Behind Gilles were several cars which had qualified ahead of him, and they wanted by. Endlessly he held Laffite, Watson, Reutemann and de Angelis at bay, making the most of his power on the one straight, keeping it precise in the tortuous corners.

Gordon Murray, of Brabham, watched the race from out on the circuit, and afterwards was almost lost for words. "That," he said, "is the greatest drive I've ever seen. That Ferrari was *terrible!* One slip by Villeneuve, and four cars would have been past him, but there wasn't the tiniest mistake..."

That race laid to rest the myth that Villeneuve was incapable of driving with discipline. As Harvey Postlethwaite said, "In terms of sheer ability, Gilles was on a different plane from the other drivers. Those two wins with the original 126 were quite out of this world – I mean, I *know* how bad that car was."

By now Postlethwaite had taken over as technical director at Ferrari, and his job it was to design a chassis capable of doing justice to the turbo V6.

"Gilles," he said, "was the most unpolitical person I've ever met. No hang-ups about anything whatsoever. In front of the Old Man, he'd say that the car was shit, that it had no downforce, and he was wasting his time. 'I'll *drive* it,' he'd say, 'because that's my job, and I love doing it. I'm just telling you that we're not going to be competitive!' Just *disarmingly* honest, and the Old Man loved him for it."

There were no more victories in 1981, but Postlethwaite's 126C2 design promised much for the following season, and Villeneuve looked forward to being more competitive.

That said, he loathed what the contemporary Grand Prix car had become. For some years 'skirts' (which achieved a seal with the ground) had been *de rigueur,* but for 1982 it was decreed they should be fixed. To avoid their being quickly destroyed, the only solution was essentially to do away with suspension movement.

At Rio, Villeneuve made his feelings plain to me. "No one outside of Formula 1 can know how bad these things are to drive. There is a moment, going over a bump and turning into a corner at the same time, when you lose vision. You don't black out exactly, but everything goes blurred. The g-forces are unbelievable. Steering is like a big truck with the power steering not working.

"After a while, your sides ache, your head aches, and you become aware of not enjoying driving a racing car – and I'm one of those guys who really *loves* driving. Thinking of some of the places we're going to this year, Zolder, I guess, will be quite a good killer, and Brands Hatch will be *something else...*

"At the moment I get a headache every time I drive the car. Now, if you make love to a woman, and at the same time someone sticks a knife in your back, eventually you won't like making love so much, right? In the same way, if you like driving, but feel your head's being punched every time you come into a corner, eventually you won't

Harvey Postlethwaite: "Gilles was the most unpolitical person I've ever met. No hang-ups about anything whatsoever. In front of the Old Man, he'd say that the car was shit, that it had no downforce, and he was wasting his time... Just disarmingly honest, and the Old Man loved him for it."

like that so much. But...take away the knife, and I still like making love!

"The cars have too much grip, so it's not spectacular, and that's not good for the spectators. They don't come to see aerodynamic brilliance – they come to be entertained, not to watch cars that look like the drivers are bedding the brakes in!"

There was another concern, too. "We're limited to two sets of qualifying tyres each, so you sit in the pits for half an hour, do a warm-up lap, and then go banzai for one lap to set a bloody time. Jesus Christ, it's dangerous! Then you find someone in your way – but you can't lift! All you can do is hope he's looking in his mirrors..."

At Imola Villeneuve came to see Pironi in his true colours. Once the Renaults had retired, Gilles and Didier were first and second, cruising, but on the last lap Pironi suddenly spurted past Villeneuve, and stole the win. On the podium, Gilles's expression said everything, and he lost no time in striding to his helicopter.

Two days later I called him in Monaco, and our conversation – an hour and more – formed the basis of a column I called 'Bad Blood at Maranello'.

Gilles was *incensed*. Forty-eight hours had done nothing to mollify him: he had been duped by someone he had trusted. I began by asking if he had discussed it with Pironi.

"No," he said, "I haven't said a word to Pironi, and I'm not going to – *ever!* I've declared war. I'll do my own thing in future. It's absolutely war...

"It was going to be my race because I was in front when we became first and second. We were very low on fuel – can you imagine a scene where two Ferraris, leading a race in Italy, ran out of fuel on the last lap?

"When he passed me the first time, I wasn't worried – I figured he was just putting on a show, impressing the fans. But what did worry me was that he was going much quicker – two seconds a lap – and the fuel thing was crucial. I got back in front and slowed the pace – but then he passed me, and picked it up again! Finally, I got by him, slowed things, and thought that was that. Then, at the last passing place on the last lap, I saw him coming up on me. I never defended myself against him, and he comes inside with wheels almost locked, and passes.

"Afterwards I thought everyone would realise what had happened, but no. Pironi said there were no team orders, and we were racing. People seemed to think we had the race of our lives! Jesus Christ, I'd been ahead of him from the start, qualified a second and a half faster than him – where was my problem? I think I've proved that, in equal cars, if I want someone to stay behind...well, I think he stays behind...

"On the podium he looked like the hero who had won, and I looked like the spoiled bastard who sulked. I know that's how it looked. OK, if I'd been beaten, I'd have been mad at myself for not going quick enough. Second place is one thing – but second because the bastard steals first, that's something else.

"People will say I'm overreacting, but I trust people until they give me reason not to – if they let me down, that's it. I would have to be very weak to shake hands, and say, 'Let's forget it'. I can't do that. This was not fourth place. This was a Grand Prix win.

"When we get to Zolder, if it's a matter of trying to pass him at the end of the straight, I'll take the same chance as if it were a Williams or a Brabham..."

At Zolder it was apparent there would be no rapprochement with Pironi. After Friday morning practice, I was chatting to Gilles when Didier drew into the pit. "Let's get out of here," he said.

The following day, in the last minutes of qualifying, the number 27 Ferrari, on a final hot lap, came up on Jochen Mass's cruising March. Mass saw Villeneuve, and moved right to give him the line, but Gilles had already committed himself to going the same way. It was like a 'plane crash.

"I flew back with Gilles after Imola," said Jackie Stewart, "and I'd never seen him angry like that. He was *stunned*. There had always been this innocence about Gilles – he didn't have a trace of malice in him, and he couldn't quite believe what had happened to him. It was awful that the last days of his life were so tormented and disillusioned."

Scheckter paid tribute to his friend: "My absolute priority was keeping myself alive, whereas it was a romantic thing for Gilles. I thought – and I will always think – that he was the fastest racing driver there has ever been, and I know there's nothing I could say that would please him more.

"If he could come back and live his life again, I'm sure he would do exactly the same – and with the same love. That's the right word, too. Gilles was in love with motor racing."

So he was. The great paradox of Gilles Villeneuve was that, if he was the most extrovert driver of a racing car that I have ever seen, out of the cockpit he was invariably the calmest of men. In it, he was the racing driver pure, with a genius that was only his.

Gilles on Imola 1982: "I thought everyone would realise what had happened, but no. Pironi said there were no team orders, and we were racing. People seemed to think we had the race of our lives! Jesus Christ, I'd been ahead of him from the start, qualified a second and a half faster...."

1967 – 1974

The motor racing career of the incomparable Gilles Villeneuve began in small-time drag and oval races with self-modified MGA and Mustang road cars. But it was snowmobile racing that nurtured the extraordinary gifts that would make him world-famous – the almost superhuman car control, the shocking bravery, the fierce will to win that thrived within him alongside a powerful sense of fair play.

He took up the sport in 1967 with his father's leisure machine, aged 17, and became a race winner

CLOCKWISE FROM RIGHT Gilles as cardboard cut-out with snowmobile trophies won in 1974; with Motoski snowmobile in 1972, the year he won the Québec championship; the two-year-old Formula Ford car with which he won seven of ten races in 1973; with his brother, Jacques, after winning at Eagle River, Wisconsin, in 1974 with his modified Alouette snowmobile; into Formula Atlantic for 1974 with an Ecurie Canada March 74B.

almost straight away. With the help of the Skiroule dealer in Berthierville, the Villeneuve family's home town in Québec, he soon became a professional snowmobile racer. After two seasons with Skiroule, he switched to the Moto-Ski firm, and the success continued. Gilles won countless snowmobile races over more than a decade. His major victories included the 440cc World Series final at Malone, New York, in 1971, the Québec championship in 1972 and – with nine wins from 10 starts – the Canadian national title in 1973.

Gilles said of the sport: "I learned many things on snowmobiles that helped me. They understeered and oversteered and you had to set up the suspension just as you would with a car. You had to build quick reactions to whatever the machine did, and you had to hang on whatever happened. Every winter, you would reckon on three or four big spills – I'm talking about being thrown on to the ice at 100mph. Those things used to slide a lot, and the visibility was terrible! Unless you were leading, you could see nothing, with all the snow blowing about. It stopped me having any worries about racing in the rain – helped me build a big heart."

Gilles was seeking some action as summer came and he couldn't race his beloved snowmobiles, when he took up car racing. He learned the rudiments in some novice races with an Alfa Romeo GTA in 1970, and then as a pupil at the Jim Russell Racing Drivers School at his local Mont Tremblant circuit near St Jovite, run by Jacques Couture. Early in 1973, he bought a two-year-old car from Jean-Pierre St Jacques, a Québecois competitor who built his own

Formula Fords. With equipment clearly inferior to cars from the established racecar brands, the techniques he had developed on the 100mph snowmobiles took him to seven wins from 10 races comprising the 1973 Québec provincial championship, run at St Jovite, Sanair and Trois-Rivières.

Gilles realised that snowmobiles would benefit from principles of racecar engineering. He acquired an Alouette frame and modified it extensively himself, fitting a wishbone suspension system. Racing against a top field, including Jacques, his younger brother, Gilles used this machine to win America's 650cc World Championship 'Derby' event in 1974 on the famous half-mile snow oval at Eagle River, Wisconsin. Gilles continued to drive snowmobiles whenever he could, and last raced one in 1981.

He and Jacques were a formidable family force in the sport. Jacques went on to build a less remarkable career in motor racing but he exceeded the achievements of his elder brother on the ice by winning the Sno Pro world championship three times on the Eagle River course, racing for Ski-Doo in 1980, 1982 and 1986. Many more snowmobile victories and championships followed.

After a single Formula Ford season, Gilles moved on to the new Canadian Formula Atlantic series in 1974. He persuaded Montréal-based Kris Harrison to give him a chance in his new Ecurie Canada team, contributing his snowmobile winnings to Harrison's budget. The Schweppes sponsorship was minimal – and Gilles trashed both the team's March chassis in pre-season testing at St Jovite. Yet he finished third in the opening round of the Player's Challenge series

at Westwood. Engine problems spoiled his next two outings, and then he crashed heavily at Mosport, breaking a leg.

Gilles missed two races and had to be lifted into his car to resume his season in Halifax. His leg was still in a cast when a first-lap collision in the non-championship Grand Prix de Trois-Rivières completed a desperately disappointing season.

Gilles lost his Ecurie Canada drive. But the first Formula Atlantic victory was not far away...

1975–1976

A SPRINGBOARD TO FAME IN ATLANTIC

Gilles couldn't raise the sponsorship to renew his Ecurie Canada drive in 1975, but found a way to continue in Formula Atlantic when he was invited to return to Skiroule's snowmobile team. He agreed on condition that Skiroule sponsored his own Atlantic programme, and ordered a March 75B. That June, in heavy rain, he broke his duck in the Player's championship with a great win at Gimli. And then, in 1976, it all came spectacularly good. After an abortive run in Mo Carter's Chevrolet Camaro in the Daytona 24 Hours, he returned to Ecurie Canada for the new Atlantic season. He won in Canada at Edmonton, Gimli, St Jovite and Halifax, and these victories were interspersed with US wins at Road America (twice), Laguna Seca and Ontario, California. With two championships in his pocket, Gilles signed off the season with a performance that stunned the visiting European stars in the big stand-alone race in the exhibition grounds at Trois-Rivières.

RIGHT Gilles's triumphant 1976 season delivered by far the most important victory of his career to date. The Trois-Rivières promoters imported a small galaxy of star drivers but, from the pole, Gilles put them all into orbit. Here he leads from Tom Klausler's Lola and the Marches of Bobby Rahal and Vittorio Brambilla.

ABOVE Gilles's self-run Atlantic team was a shoestring operation and the first two races were won by Ecurie Canada's new driver, Bertil Roos. But Gilles then produced a startling drive in driving rain to win the 1975 Winnipeg Grand Prix at Gimli – from 19th on the grid. He finished second at St Jovite (pictured), drove the fastest lap at Mosport, and wound up fifth in the championship. At season's end, against the visiting European stars at Trois-Rivières, he qualified third behind Patrick Depailler and Jean-Pierre Jarier, ahead of Vittorio Brambilla, Jose Dolhem and Jean-Pierre Jaussaud. Fading brakes caused a crash after he had run second. Gilles thanked Skiroule for its support by winning 32 of 36 snowmobile races contested over the following winter...

RIGHT Gilles raced in Europe for the first time in June 1976, as a component of a French-Canadian joint promotion by the street race organisers in the towns of Trois-Rivières and Pau. A Formula 2 drive was arranged at the historic French venue with Ron Dennis's newly formed Project Four team, whose March 762s were underpowered. Arriving with four Atlantic wins from the first five races, Gilles seized the opportunity aggressively, spinning regularly but qualifying 10th, half a second quicker than his much-touted team mate, Eddie Cheever. His race ended early with an overheated engine. The Grand Prix de Pau was dominated by future Formula 1 rivals: René Arnoux won from Jacques Laffite, Jean-Pierre Jabouille and Jean-Pierre Jarier.

LEFT Having impressed the new Ecurie Canada team manager, Ray Wardell, a former March Formula 1 engineer, Gilles was entered in CASC's 1976 Canadian Atlantic series and IMSA's American championship, and dominated both. Then he defeated allcomers in the Grand Prix de Trois-Rivières. Here he sets out on the formation lap with Tom Klausler's Lola alongside and Bobby Rahal's March tucked in behind. Patrick Tambay is in the blue Chevron, and James Hunt in the red March.

BELOW A new name is in the world's motor racing headlines. Gilles enjoys his moments on the rostrum at Trois-Rivières.

LEFT Gilles heads for the victory that changed his life. His opponents at Trois-Rivières included Alan Jones, James Hunt (in another Ecurie Canada March), Vittorio Brambilla, Bobby Rahal and Patrick Tambay. Hunt, who was *en route* to his 1976 World Championship, was hugely impressed. Visiting the US Grand Prix at Watkins Glen that October, Gilles was introduced to Teddy Mayer, the principal of the McLaren Formula 1 team, and John Hogan of Marlboro, its title sponsor. Later he was summoned to England and offered a contract to drive in up to five Grands Prix in 1977 in a third McLaren, alongside Hunt and Jochen Mass. Mayer also took out an option on his services for 1978.

1977

F1 DEBUTS FOR McLAREN AND FERRARI

Gilles found himself in a frantic defence of his Canadian Atlantic championship in 1977, under extreme pressure from such as Keke Rosberg. His tenacity delivered the title again, but his domestic series had become almost a distraction before season's end. He had accepted the offer of a Can-Am drive with Walter Wolf's team, managed by Chris Amon, and made his début immediately after undergoing a McLaren Formula 1 test in England. He then competed in his maiden Grand Prix and impressed everyone at Silverstone, but McLaren decided not to retain him. Gilles was devastated. He returned home – and was startled to get a telephone call from Ferrari. Amon, among others, had urged Enzo Ferrari to give Gilles a chance. Ultimately he was entered for the season-closing Grands Prix in Canada and Japan. At Fuji, Gilles had an appalling accident which cost the lives of two onlookers. However the Scuderia had seen the potential, and retained him for the following season.

RIGHT Gilles's Silverstone test with McLaren. He had never seen the circuit, nor driven anything more powerful than his 2-litre Atlantic cars, but he tackled the opportunity in the cavalier style that would become his hallmark. He alarmed Teddy Mayer's team by spinning often – but seldom twice in the same place...

LEFT Gilles accepted an offer to race a works Chevron in January and February 1977 in a four-race international Formula Atlantic series in South Africa, to find that the new B39 was not yet competitive against the March 77B. The first three races were dominated by Ian Scheckter, and Gilles could muster only a third at Cape Town (pictured, leading Rupert Keegan's March) and a fifth at Kyalami. The venture ended with a battery failure at Welkom and then a heavy accident at Port Elizabeth when Scheckter spun his March and Gilles, unsighted, T-boned it. The March rolled and caught fire with its driver trapped beneath, but Gilles was able to haul Scheckter clear.

LEFT Ecurie Canada became the official engine supplier to CASC's Labatt's Formula Atlantic championship in 1977 and, for political reasons, competed by forming an offshoot team, named Motor Racing Company of Canada. Gilles's March 77B was managed by Dave Morris, a Canadian Formula Ford champion who had quit racing in 1974 after his abandoned Atlantic March was struck by Gilles in the Mosport accident that broke his leg. This time, Gilles had to scrap to win the title against much more formidable opposition, including Keke Rosberg in Fred Opert's works-supported Chevron. A spectacular, wheel-banging duel between these two at Mosport ended with both cars off the track and Gilles could finish only second to Price Cobb's March. Bobby Rahal's Truesports March won at Gimli after Gilles lost his engine, and he had to wait until Edmonton for his first victory – after another sensational battle with Rosberg.

BELOW Gilles was tested by McLaren at a two-day FOCA test at Silverstone 10 days before the 1977 British Grand Prix, with an M23 previously raced by 1976 World Champion James Hunt. Here he shares a joke in pit lane with McLaren team manager Alistair Caldwell.

ABOVE Gilles flew from his Formula 1 test in England directly to Watkins Glen in New York state, where he did the first of four races in the SCCA's revived, 5-litre Can-Am series. Canadian entrant Walter Wolf had ordered a Chevrolet-powered car from the Italian manufacturer, Dallara. It turned out to be a dog and its original driver, Chris Amon, opted out of its cockpit after only one race, taking up the team management role. Here Amon (at left, hand on chin) looks on as Gilles prepares to qualify the ill-handling Wolf Dallara in fourth position.

RIGHT Joann, Gilles's wife of almost seven years, seems to need reassurance in pit lane at Silverstone for his first race meeting as a Grand Prix driver.

JOHN PLAYER GRAND PRIX
SEE Motor EVERY WEEK Motor
Marlboro
Marlboro
TEXACO
Marlboro
TEAM McLAREN
Marlboro
40
GOODYEAR
12

LEFT Pictured during Saturday practice at Silverstone, Gilles was entered in a McLaren M23 alongside the new M26s of James Hunt and Jochen Mass. After negotiating a pre-qualifying session that reduced a 40-car entry, he startled the Formula 1 community by qualifying ninth, only 0.43sec away from Hunt's pole position time, and 0.23sec ahead of Mass. He covered no fewer than 169 laps over three days, spinning frequently. He remarked afterwards: "For me, the quickest way to learn the limits of the M23 was to go quicker and quicker through each corner until it spun. Then I knew how quick was too quick. By the end of Saturday, it felt like I was driving an Atlantic car with an extra-powerful engine, so now I could throw the McLaren around a bit." Passing by is Carlos Reutemann's Ferrari.

ABOVE The first Formula 1 start is a couple of minutes away. Hunt's McLaren M26 and John Watson's Brabham-Alfa lead the British Grand Prix formation lap on Silverstone's Hangar Straight, followed by Jody Scheckter's Wolf, Niki Lauda's Ferrari, the Lotus 78s of Gunnar Nilsson (left) and Mario Andretti, Hans Stuck's Brabham and Vittorio Brambilla's white Surtees. Gilles is next in his M23, having outqualified Ronnie Peterson's Tyrrell P34 and Mass's newer M26. Tucked up behind Carlos Reutemann's Ferrari is Gilles's friend Patrick Tambay, who also started a Formula 1 race for the first time here at the wheel of an Ensign. The second of the yellow cars is Jean-Pierre Jabouille's Renault, making the first Grand Prix start by a turbocharged engine.

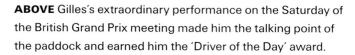

ABOVE Gilles's extraordinary performance on the Saturday of the British Grand Prix meeting made him the talking point of the paddock and earned him the 'Driver of the Day' award.

RIGHT Gilles went from ninth on the grid straight into seventh position in his maiden Formula 1 race and was still there when his water temperature gauge went off the clock. He pitted at the end of the 10th lap and lost two laps while his crew established that the gauge was faulty. He rejoined in a cloud of tyre smoke, circulated with the leading group for the duration of the British Grand Prix, and was classified 11th.

ABOVE LEFT The Can-Am at Mosport Park in August 1977 was in a double-header with the Mosport 6 Hours, a round of the World Championship of Makes run on the Saturday. Gilles accepted a drive in this BMW 320i, operated by Rudi Faltz's team out of Germany. It was his only endurance race, and the first for his co-driver, Eddie Cheever. Cheever broke a driveshaft early in practice, so Gilles didn't get to drive the car until the race. They won Group 5 and finished third overall behind a Porsche 934 raced by Ludwig Heimrath and Paul Miller, but were later promoted to second place after the winning Porsche of Peter Gregg and Bob Wollek was disqualified due to a suspension infringement. McLaren North America ran its 320i turbo in this race but Ronnie Peterson and David Hobbs were hampered by an oil leak and finished second in Group 5, far behind the naturally aspirated Faltz entry.

BELOW LEFT Gilles hands the BMW back to Cheever during the routine pitstop after the second stint. Later he drove the last 90 minutes in very humid conditions, and then fainted on the podium. He quickly recovered but, that evening, he was dismayed when Teddy Mayer told him the McLaren Formula 1 team would not be taking up its option for 1978. Marlboro had no market in Canada. Frenchman Patrick Tambay was preferred as Jochen Mass's replacement.

LEFT The week after Mosport, Gilles received a telephone call from Ferrari, and within days he found himself in Maranello. It certainly tempered his dejection after losing his 1978 drive to Patrick Tambay, one of his Can-Am rivals with whom he had struck up a good friendship. Back in Canada for the Trois-Rivières double-header, he is pictured with Tambay in the Can-Am assembly area. In the race, Gilles lost his engine, and Tambay bagged the fourth of six victories with Carl Haas's works Lola that delivered the title.

ABOVE As the 1977 Can-Am season progressed, the Wolf Dallara sprouted a nose wing, a reduced rear wing and bigger cooling ducts as Chris Amon's team struggled to give Gilles a car that worked. Attacking the turns in his inimitable style, he generally qualified well but finished only one race, third at Road America after starting from pole. The recalcitrant car jammed itself in fourth gear, and broke its engine here at Trois-Rivières. The following week, Gilles was back in Italy, where he began negotiating a release from his McLaren contract during the Formula 1 meeting at Monza, and tested a Ferrari at Fiorano.

RIGHT Gilles hurls his MRCC March at a turn on the Trois-Rivières street circuit. His scintillating lap-time delivered pole position for the 1977 Formula Atlantic race, a whole second quicker than a group comprising visiting French stars Patrick Depailler and Jacques Laffite in Fred Opert's Chevrons, Price Cobb and Keke Rosberg. His race was frantic, however. He and Rosberg tangled in the first corner, putting Keke's Chevron into the wall. Gilles regained the lead from Depailler but, restarting after a late-race yellow, he collided with Cobb and was clobbered by Laffite. He finished a frustrated fourth behind Cobb, Howdy Holmes and Depailler.

ABOVE Newly invited to Italy by Enzo Ferrari, Gilles suppresses his excitement as he concentrates on the start of the 1977 Grand Prix de Québec. After winning the race, Gilles went to Maranello, accompanied by his friend and mentor, Gaston Parent, and was offered a drive with the world's most famous Grand Prix team. "If someone had told me I could have three wishes," Gilles said, "my first would have been to get into racing, my second to be in Formula 1, and my third to drive for Ferrari..."

RIGHT Canadian fans still talk about the torrid battles between Gilles's white March and Keke Rosberg's pink Chevron during the 1977 Canadian Atlantic series, which ended here with the Grand Prix de Québec in the city's exhibition grounds. Rosberg had won at Westwood when Gilles was otherwise engaged at Silverstone, and now the title fight was effectively between them and Bill Brack. Gilles badly damaged his March in qualifying when he couldn't avoid Tom Gloy's spinning March, and then crashed team mate Richard Spenard's car in his desperation to retrieve pole position. He started third on the grid behind his rival contenders, but both were involved in accidents and, after a duel with Bobby Rahal, Gilles won. It was only his third victory from a much more competitive season, his 13th from 26 starts in Formula Atlantic, and his final race in the category.

LEFT After returning from Italy with a Ferrari contract in his pocket, Gilles watched from the Scuderia's pit as Niki Lauda clinched the 1977 championship at Watkins Glen. He was entered for the Canadian Grand Prix the following weekend in a third 312T2, alongside Lauda and Carlos Reutemann. However, tensions finally came to a head between the team and its new champion, who had signed a 1978 contract with Brabham. On the Friday morning, Lauda told the media he was fed up with Ferrari polemics and it was crazy to run a third car. He stormed out of the circuit and flew home to Austria. It was a good decision in terms of Ferrari's competitiveness here. Both the remaining drivers struggled for grip, and Reutemann qualified 12th with Gilles 17th, half a second slower after trashing his car's rear suspension in the final session.

ABOVE On his debut for Ferrari, in front of his home crowd, Gilles endures the ignominy of being lapped by Canadian Grand Prix winner Jody Scheckter's Wolf. Gilles spent some of the race battling with Patrick Tambay's Ensign and was running in eighth place when he spun, seven laps from the finish. Four laps later, he spun again on oil that had already accounted for three other cars and, in resuming, vented his frustration on a driveshaft. He was classified 12th.

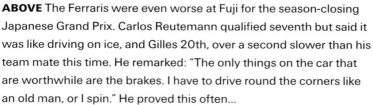

ABOVE The Ferraris were even worse at Fuji for the season-closing Japanese Grand Prix. Carlos Reutemann qualified seventh but said it was like driving on ice, and Gilles 20th, over a second slower than his team mate this time. He remarked: "The only things on the car that are worthwhile are the brakes. I have to drive round the corners like an old man, or I spin." He proved this often...

RIGHT Fuji-san looks on as Gilles tiptoes his gripless Ferrari round Fuji International Speedway. His race ended in a dreadful tragedy after six laps when what he claimed was a brake failure sent him into the back of Ronnie Peterson's Tyrrell at the end of the long start-finish straight. The Ferrari went airborne and, shedding bodywork, wheels and wings, cartwheeled over a barrier and deep into a prohibited zone that was crowded with photographers and spectators. Two people – a photographer and a marshal who was trying to clear the area – were killed, and seven injured. Gilles remained strapped into what was left of the monocoque and stepped out unhurt. "I felt sad about the people who were killed," he said later, "but I didn't feel responsible for the deaths. I knew they were standing in a forbidden area."

1978

A DREAM COMES TRUE
IN MONTREAL

Gilles's first full season as a Formula 1 driver came in 1978, racing the new Ferrari 312T3 as the team mate of the experienced Carlos Reutemann. The latest flat-12 design from Maranello turned out to be the second-best chassis in a season dominated by the innovative, ground-effect Lotus 79. Yet Ferrari's performances were mostly remarkable for their inconsistency. Michelin's new radial tyres were quick on some circuits, devoid of grip on others, and usually incapable of maintaining pace over full race distances. This curious, hit-and-miss season delivered Gilles's first fastest lap (in Buenos Aires with an updated 1977 car), his first championship points (at Zolder), his first podium (on the Osterreichring) – and his first victory. And it came in his home Canadian Grand Prix in Montreal, where he was able to use his wonderful wet-weather skills to full advantage. "The happiest day of my life!" Gilles called it. "To win your first Grand Prix at home is completely unthinkable..."

RIGHT Gilles's Ferrari 312T2 leads Patrick Tambay's McLaren M26 during the opening Grand Prix in Buenos Aires. It took Tambay until the 43rd of the 52 laps to find a way past. He went on to finish sixth. Gilles was eighth behind Carlos Reutemann, who had been delayed by a pitstop.

ABOVE LEFT Gilles consults with a Michelin engineer at Long Beach. The new 312T3, designed for Ferrari's switch from Goodyear crossply tyres to Michelin radials, had had a disappointing debut in the previous race at Kyalami. It was transformed for the US Grand Prix West by the arrival of new tyres.

ABOVE Gilles leads Vittorio Brambilla's Surtees out of the Queens hairpin at Long Beach. The much-improved red cars qualified on the front row in California, with Carlos Reutemann on the pole. Gilles led the race until halfway but misjudged the pass when he came up to lap Clay Regazzoni's Shadow and Jean-Pierre Jabouille's Renault. He was pitched into the wall by contact with the former. Reutemann drove past to the win.

LEFT Out of the race and now a grumpy spectator, Gilles reclines on one of the concrete blocks that served as temporary (and unforgiving) barriers. "Now I know what it's like to lead the first half of a race," Gilles said later. "So now I want the other half..."

NEXT PAGE Fresh Michelins are mounted on Gilles's Ferrari in the Monaco pit lane. Carlos Reutemann qualified on the pole here with Gilles more than a second slower, first time out on the track on the streets where he and Joann now lived. "A good mountain circuit with a town around it," Gilles called it. "Every corner is different, and delicate." Reutemann made contact with Niki Lauda's Brabham-Alfa in the first turn and punctured a tyre, but Gilles upheld Ferrari honour for most of the distance.

LEFT Emerson Fittipaldi makes room for Gilles to lap him at the Loews hairpin during the Monaco Grand Prix. Wowing the crowd with his sideways driving, Gilles ascended from eighth on the grid to fourth place but, as he sped through the tunnel for the 63rd time, his left front tyre surrendered, and abruptly deflated. The car emerged from the mouth of the tunnel on three wheels after a heavy impact with the barrier.

ABOVE Gilles speeds towards his best Formula 1 performance – and result – to date. He overshadowed his team mate in the Belgian Grand Prix at Zolder, holding a strong second place behind Mario Andretti, who was débuting the very classy Lotus 79, until a front tyre punctured as he embarked on his 40th lap. He drove hard after the pitstop and finished a worthy fourth, only 23sec astern of Carlos Reutemann. "Points!" Gilles smiled. "Finally!"

RIGHT Red formation in Sweden. Gilles and 'Lole' were dismayed when their Ferraris handled so poorly on the Anderstorp circuit, as they had in hot weather conditions in the previous race at Jarama. Suddenly almost 2sec off the pace, they could qualify only seventh and eighth, and finish only ninth and tenth in a race won by Niki Lauda in the outrageous Brabham-Alfa 'fan-car'.

VI SKA GE SVERIGES BIL
GB
TRICO
Lucas
AMPS
BilAtlas
MICHELIN
Agip
11
42
HEUER

RIGHT Gilles runs his Ferrari up the kerbing on the exit of the St Baume sequence of turns, and embarks on the long trip down the awesome Mistrale straightaway that characterised the Paul Ricard circuit at Le Castellet. Ahead of him is Patrick Depailler's Tyrrell 008. Both the red cars again struggled for grip in this race, and both were delayed by pitstops for fresh rubber.

LEFT A rear wing adjustment for the T3 in the crowded pit lane at Brands Hatch for the British Grand Prix. Michelin brought new front tyres to this race but Gilles mistakenly stuck with the old. He qualified three rows behind Carlos Reutemann and pitted for the new tyres after only 10 laps. He went out with a broken driveshaft only nine laps after rejoining but, after the Lotus 79s had dropped out, 'Lole' won.

ABOVE Gilles and Ronnie Peterson are interviewed on the podium after the Austrian Grand Prix. This race was stopped after only seven laps by a cloudburst. After the restart, Gilles came through to finish third, a distance behind Peterson's winning Lotus and overtaken by Patrick Depailler's Tyrrell. It was the first podium of his Formula 1 career. "The rain didn't worry me," he said. "I think I like it better than when it's dry."

LEFT The drive that endeared him to the whole of Italy. Four days before he was due to drive a Ferrari at Monza for the first time, after a lot of negative media speculation, the team renewed Gilles's contract for 1979. He immediately rewarded its trust in him. He was outqualified only by Mario Andretti's Lotus 79, and led off the line. But the race was stopped after the 10-car accident that mortally injured Andretti's team mate, Gilles's hero, Ronnie Peterson. At the long-delayed restart, Gilles took off again, and Andretti needed 34 laps of the reduced 40-lap distance to find a way past him. Gilles showed the fans all his tenacity in his pursuit of the far superior Lotus and finished only 2sec behind it. Then both men were penalised 60sec for jumping the start, handing Niki Lauda and John Watson a 1-2 for Brabham and Alfa Romeo. Gilles's penalty dropped him to seventh, but this seemed unimportant. He said: "Ronnie's death has hit me hard. I've always admired him as one of the quickest drivers around. I don't think about dying, but I accept that the risk is part of the job."

LEFT Gilles arrived in Montréal for his home Grand Prix without much to shout about – a fourth in Belgium, a third in Austria, disappointments otherwise. It was all about to change...

RIGHT Rain gave the Formula 1 circus a soggy introduction to the Circuit Ile Notre-Dame. Gilles loved this. He qualified third behind Jean-Pierre Jarier (Ronnie Peterson's successor at Team Lotus) and Jody Scheckter in the Wolf. He lost out on the first lap to Alan Jones in his Williams FW06 but recovered third place on lap 19, and went second on lap 26. He could make no impression on Jarier, but soon the Lotus was parked by a brake fluid leak. Gilles found himself with a handsome lead. But, he recalled later: "Those last laps were torture! It was easy when I was trying to put pressure on Jarier – quick-shifting, braking hard, on full power in the corners. I love charging and I try to put on a show. But then I had to drive like an old woman, just being careful not to break anything, and I could hear all kinds of noises in the car."

LEFT Gilles held on to win from Scheckter and Reutemann, one year after his Ferrari début here. The team mates are joined on the podium by Joann as Gilles's brother, Jacques (at left), looks on with Canadian prime minister Pierre Trudeau. Gilles had stopped at the finish-line after his slowdown lap, and taken the chequered flag on a victory lap. Later he did a trade with the race starter, Michel Hanson, to keep the flag that had signalled his maiden Formula 1 victory, in return for a large Ferrari flag from Maranello.

1979

A TRIPLE WINNER IN A FERRARI 1-2

With Carlos Reutemann gone to Team Lotus for the 1979 season, Jody Scheckter came to Scuderia Ferrari after two seasons with Wolf. He and Gilles were equipped with the frumpish 312T4, a new car designed to exploit the emerging science of ground-effect aerodynamics as much as possible within the limitations imposed by the team's wide, flat-12 engine. Optimised for Michelin's radial tyres, the 515bhp T4 was both powerful and durable, and it romped the Constructors' championship. Each man won three races over the course of the season. Scheckter led 170 racing laps, Gilles 308. Jody drove one fastest lap, Gilles five. But Jody scored points in 12 of the 15 races, Gilles in only eight. So Jody won the title and Gilles was the runner-up. "I just didn't get the breaks," he shrugged after it was over. "Jody did. That's the way it goes in motor racing..." It was the closest he ever came to being the world champion.

RIGHT This famous photograph sums up the unforgettable spirit of the man. Gilles led at Zandvoort until a deflating rear tyre put him into multiple, smoky spins. Two laps later, the tyre blew apart at Tarzan, the first corner. He raced back to pit lane. When he got there, the back of his Ferrari was trashed.

LEFT The Scuderia's hardware at the opening race in Buenos Aires was the ineffectual T3 as used in 1978, but the DFV opposition had moved on. Jody Scheckter (at right) qualified fifth but Gilles's pre-race programme was hampered by a fuel-feed fault and he never came fully to grips with his car, lining it up in 10th position. Beyond Scheckter, team director Mauro Forghieri confers with newly recruited engineer Antonio Tomaini.

ABOVE All Ferrari's hopes were pinned on Gilles after Scheckter had been eliminated in a multiple first-lap shunt that stopped the Argentine Grand Prix. But Gilles never rose above sixth place after the restart before his engine broke four laps out from the finish.

NEXT PAGE The 312T4 showed a lot of promise in testing and the Scuderia debuted it in the third race of the 1979 season at Kyalami, where the altitude assisted the first pole position for Jean-Pierre Jabouille's turbo V6 Renault. Gilles lost the final hour of qualifying after the team discovered a cracked rear suspension mounting point on the new car, but he put it third on the grid behind his team mate. Both Ferraris got the drop on the Renault and Niki Lauda's Brabham at the start of the race.

RIGHT Kyalami, lap two. A sudden cloudburst caused the South African Grand Prix to be red-flagged when Gilles was already holding a substantial lead. After the restart, Gilles started on grooved tyres, Scheckter on slicks, and the track surface dried quickly. Gilles led the first 14 laps as the Scuderia established a 1-2, and was the last of 20 drivers to stop for slicks. Scheckter's run was later interrupted when a locking brake flat-spotted his tyres and Gilles went past him again while he was in pit lane.

ABOVE Gilles, right arm raised in triumph, crosses the finish-line at Kyalami, still 3sec and more in front of his South African team mate.

LEFT Gilles celebrates his victory after a debut 1-2 success for the Ferrari T4. Jean-Pierre Jarier, placed third with his Tyrrell, tries to get some fizz out of his Moët.

RIGHT Gilles arrived in Long Beach and slid off the track on his second lap on Friday morning. The Ferrari was repaired over the lunch break and he was second fastest in the qualifying session that afternoon. On the Saturday, he used Michelin's softest to achieve his first Formula 1 pole position.

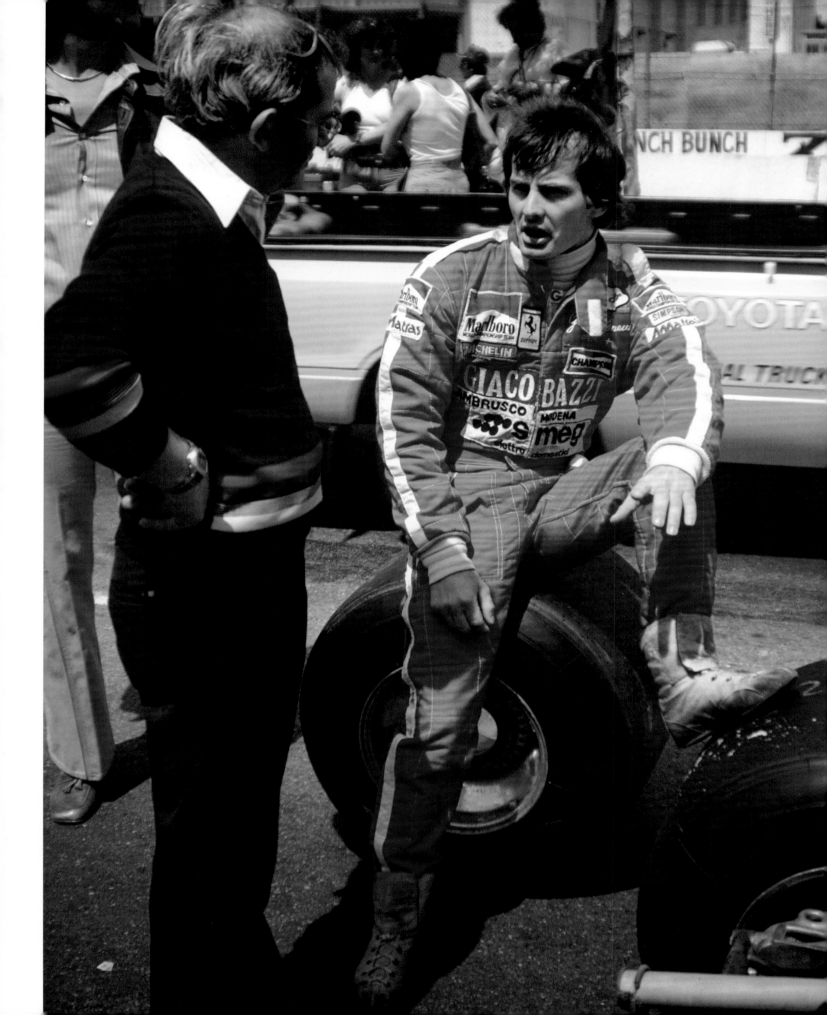

LEFT Gilles drove the pole position lap at Long Beach with a gearbox-mounted rear wing on his Ferrari T4, going eight-hundredths of a second quicker than team mate Jody Scheckter. For the race, he decided to revert to the standard configuration. Scheckter opted for the forward-mounted wing.

LEFT Gilles has the inside line as the Ferraris arrive at the end of Shoreline Drive ahead of Patrick Depailler's Ligier, Mario Andretti's Lotus, James Hunt's Wolf and the rest. Seems Californian track workers were allowed to stand on top of those concrete barriers... Gilles made good his escape after Scheckter had been overtaken by Depailler and Jean-Pierre Jarier with his Tyrrell. Jody took a while to retrieve second place and had no hope of catching Gilles, who set lap and race records *en route* to the Scuderia's second successive 1-2. "People said I was lucky in Montréal because Jarier dropped out, and lucky at Kyalami with the tyre situation," Gilles said. "But whatever they say now, this one was all mine."

ABOVE Jody congratulates Gilles after his Long Beach success, which put him into the lead of the championship. At left on the podium is Alan Jones, who had finished a fighting third, last time out with the Williams FW06. Those lovely Lubri Lon ladies were promoting a brand of oil additive that was the title sponsor of the race.

RIGHT Gilles bullies his Ferrari onto the Grand Prix loop at Brands Hatch on his way to winning the Race of Champions by the best part of half a minute from Nelson Piquet's Brabham-Alfa, with Mario Andretti's Lotus a fading third.

NEXT PAGE Angry with himself for allowing Carlos Reutemann past on the second lap of the Spanish Grand Prix at Jarama, Gilles spoiled his chances with a smoky spin when he took an ill-advised lunge at the Lotus two laps later, and was narrowly avoided by his team mate. He resumed in eighth place but spun again at the same corner next time around, dropping to 13th. After that, seventh was the best he could do.

LEFT Pictured in pit lane at Zolder, the Ferrari 312T4 looks tinny, but it represented the state of the Formula 1 art in 1979. Gilles came to the Belgian Grand Prix sharing the lead of the championship with Ligier's Patrick Depailler.

RIGHT It rained on the Friday morning at Zolder, and Gilles completed many more laps than any other driver. As the surface dried out during the afternoon qualifying session, all that track time paid off with the provisional pole position. But Michelin's qualifying tyres were no match for Goodyear's softest rubber here when the surface was bone-dry on the Saturday, and he slipped to sixth on the grid. On the second lap of the race, he couldn't avoid Clay Regazzoni's Williams when it got tangled up with the other Ferrari, and struck it hard enough to shred his nosecone. A new nose was fitted in the pits and Gilles, restarting dead last, produced his most spectacular Formula 1 drive to date. A stunning performance took him all the way to third place – and then his T4 ran out of fuel a few hundred yards from the finish-line. Jody Scheckter's victory took him into the series lead.

ABOVE Gilles and Jody Scheckter (at right) would often drive together to Fiorano to test the 312T4 on the Scuderia's private circuit. On this occasion, they had company when they stopped for a break in a layby, but it looks like they declined to give the lady a lift. Gilles was a dedicated test driver. Ferrari records show that he covered more than 37,000 miles in 1978-79 at Fiorano alone.

RIGHT On track together, as so often in 1979, Jody and Gilles hurry down the hill towards the Portier corner at Monaco. Apart from a brief incursion between them by Niki Lauda's Brabham, they held down a 1-2 all the way to lap 54.

NEXT PAGE Gilles in Casino Square at Monaco. His run was halted by a transmission breakage and team mate Jody Scheckter was left alone to secure a narrow victory over Clay Regazzoni, charging hard for Williams.

LEFT Enzo Ferrari considered the T4 to be the ugliest Formula 1 racecar ever to emerge from his factory at Maranello. Here is Gilles, understeering into the Station hairpin at Monaco. He loved racing there: "The chicane is just a blur! Every time you go in there, you think – wow! I'm going to crash! Then – shoom, zap, it's gone! Around the Piscine, I was going very quickly but I could see the crowd was appreciating what I was doing. You barely see it, but it does register. It was a good feeling."

ABOVE The start of the sensational 1979 French Grand Prix, and Gilles outdrags the turbocharged Renaults of Jean-Pierre Jabouille and René Arnoux, which had annexed the front row at Dijon-Prénois, almost taking Jody Scheckter with him to the front of the race. Gilles led until after halfway but then, with deteriorating tyres, had no answer when Jabouille really turned it on with the more powerful Renault. Arnoux recovered from his poor start and chased Gilles down with four laps remaining, and suddenly the two found themselves fighting one of the most famous battles in Formula 1 history.

ABOVE RIGHT Over the final three laps of the French Grand Prix, his tyres rooted, locking up in the turns in clouds of white smoke, Gilles wrestled with Arnoux for every inch of track and sometimes the grass verge. Rubbing wheels more than once, they changed places four times on the last lap alone, and the Ferrari was just ahead at the chequer.

RIGHT To Jabouille, the spoils of his maiden Grand Prix victory – also the first in Formula 1 for Renault, and the first for a turbocharged engine. Gilles looks somewhat bemused after his torrid duel with Arnoux.

RIGHT The two protagonists of the brief but never-to-be-forgotten 'war' at Dijon, pictured together earlier in the season, at Kyalami. Gilles and René Arnoux, pocket-sized Grand Prix racers both, were already good mates and the duel cemented a mutual respect. Gilles said of it: "It was really fun. Those laps were just fantastic, the two of us outbraking each other, touching each other. I thought for sure we were going to get on our heads because, when you start interlocking wheels, it's so easy for one car to climb over the other. But we didn't crash. So – OK. I enjoyed it amazingly!" They were firmly united against the criticism that followed from their fellow drivers, calling it: "Completely stupid."

ABOVE Unfortunately for Scuderia Ferrari, it was the turn of Silverstone to host the 1979 British Grand Prix under the alternating arrangement with Brands Hatch. The scarcity of slow turns on the featureless airfield circuit eliminated the torque advantage of the flat-12 engine, and neither of the team's men could get on a front-running pace. Jody Scheckter qualified 11th, Gilles 13th.

RIGHT Lap 50 of the British Grand Prix. Gilles hustled his T4 into fourth place but now he has caused consternation in the Ferrari pits by his unannounced arrival, having heard a strange noise from his engine. He rejoined but the car was parked by a fuel-feed fault 13 laps later. This race delivered the maiden Formula 1 victory for the Williams team, with Clay Regazzoni. Scheckter was fifth.

LEFT Gilles in pit lane at the Osterreichring with two of his best friends in racing, Patrick Tambay and Jody Scheckter. The Frenchman had stayed on at Marlboro Team McLaren but, 10 races into the 1979 championship, had yet to score a point. Gilles and Jody had 61 between them with the reliable Ferraris. The two found they worked well together, always ready to share information and to help each other. In May 1982 Jody would deliver the eulogy at Gilles's funeral in Berthierville, describing him as: "The fastest racing driver in history."

RIGHT The Osterreichring road circuit in the Styrian hills was very nearly as fast as Silverstone, and again Ferrari's drivers struggled in qualifying. But Gilles made what was described as the best Formula 1 start for a decade, surging forward from fifth on the grid to lead the pack up the hill towards the big Hella-Licht S-bend that started the awesome, 3.7-mile lap. Alan Jones in the white Williams, Niki Lauda in the red Brabham and René Arnoux in the pole position Renault must have thought Gilles had jumped the start, but he hadn't. Gilles was passed during the opening 10 laps by both Jones and Arnoux, but finished second after René had to make a late stop for fuel.

LEFT Williams FW07 driver Alan Jones leads Gilles on the opening lap of the Dutch Grand Prix, followed by Jean-Pierre Jabouille (Renault) and Didier Pironi (Tyrrell), then Jacques Laffite (Ligier) and Keke Rosberg (Wolf). Gilles's lightning start from sixth on the grid led to four-abreast mayhem in the first corner, where René Arnoux's pole position Renault collided with Clay Regazzoni's Williams. Arnoux can be seen exiting the big Tarzan hairpin, headed for retirement with deranged rear suspension, and Regazzoni at the apex of the turn minus his left front wheel. Jody Scheckter is only just coming into the picture after an overheated clutch destroyed his start.

ABOVE Gilles went past Jones and into the lead after 10 laps, and held it until a deflating rear tyre sent him into multiple, smoky spins under braking for the chicane 36 laps later. Two laps after that, the tyre blew apart as he passed the pits, sending him off the track at Tarzan, the first corner. For Gilles, it was never over until the car couldn't move any more. Gille's DNF here, and Scheckter's eventual second place behind Jones, made the South African the Scuderia's title contender. "The turning point between us," Gilles called it.

NEXT PAGE After 12 laps at Monza, the Ferraris were running first and second, and Gilles had himself firmly planted between his team mate and Jacques Laffite, the closest challenger for the championship. It stayed like this until the 42nd of 50 laps, when the Ligier was halted by a blown engine, caused by a jammed clutch. That did it for Jody: he was the new champion, and he had clinched it by leading a Ferrari 1-2 on the Autodromo Nazionale. Afterwards Gilles remarked: "It wasn't a present for Jody, you know. I was trying hard." No one was fooled.

LEFT Some of the teams stayed in Italy after Monza to contest a non-championship race the following weekend at Imola. Ferrari celebrated its double by sending two cars, and they monopolised the front row, with Gilles on the pole. Gilles led the first 20 laps but then the Ferraris were struggling for grip and were passed by Niki Lauda. Only Gilles kept up the fight but, in trying to repass Lauda, he hit him and had to pit for a new nose. So the Gran Premio Dino Ferrari was won by a Brabham with Alfa Romeo power. Jody finished third behind Carlos Reutemann's Lotus 79. On fresh tyres, Gilles further endeared himself to the Italian fans with a spectacular charge. He repeatedly drove fastest laps and unlapped himself, but finished seventh.

BELOW Gilles was back in Italy in October 1979, co-opted onto the Fiat group's factory Lancia team for the Giro d'Italia, and sharing one of its turbocharged, 1.4-litre Montecarlo Group 5 cars with rally specialists Walter Röhrl and Christian Geistdörfer. As well as tarmac special stages and hillclimbs, the 1416-mile event included eight races. Gilles did the first four before departing to test his Formula 1 Ferrari at Paul Ricard. It was enough to establish the overall lead, which his co-drivers maintained to the finish. Riccardo Patrese/Markku Alen/Ilkka Kivimaki came in second with the other Lancia but both cars were later disqualified for deviating from the official route.

LEFT Gilles was taken aback by the attention lavished on him by the Canadian media and public on his return to Montréal. "I can't wait to get in the car," he said. "It will be quiet there..." It wasn't. After sharing the front row of the grid, Gilles and Alan Jones battled furiously from the start of the Canadian Grand Prix all the way to the finish. The Ferrari had the advantage for the first 50 laps before the increasingly effective Williams was scrabbled into the lead at the hairpin. Jones remained under unrelenting pressure, but led for the remaining 22 laps.

ABOVE Jones holds Gilles's arm aloft after being astounded by his never-say-die pursuit on the Ile Notre Dame. The result meant that second place in the championship would go to the wire at Watkins Glen.

NEXT PAGE Advantage, Villeneuve: the start of the US Grand Prix, and it's raining. Gilles's fantastic wet-weather skills had already been the talk of Watkins Glen, where the first qualifying session had also been run on a very wet track. One of only six drivers venturing out from pit lane, he had been fastest by more than 10 seconds... On a dry surface, he had qualified third in the second session, but now the weather has brought the race to him. By putting two wheels on the treacherous grass verge at the first corner, Gilles has monstered his way into the lead and is ahead of his rivals for second place in the championship, Alan Jones and Jacques Laffite.

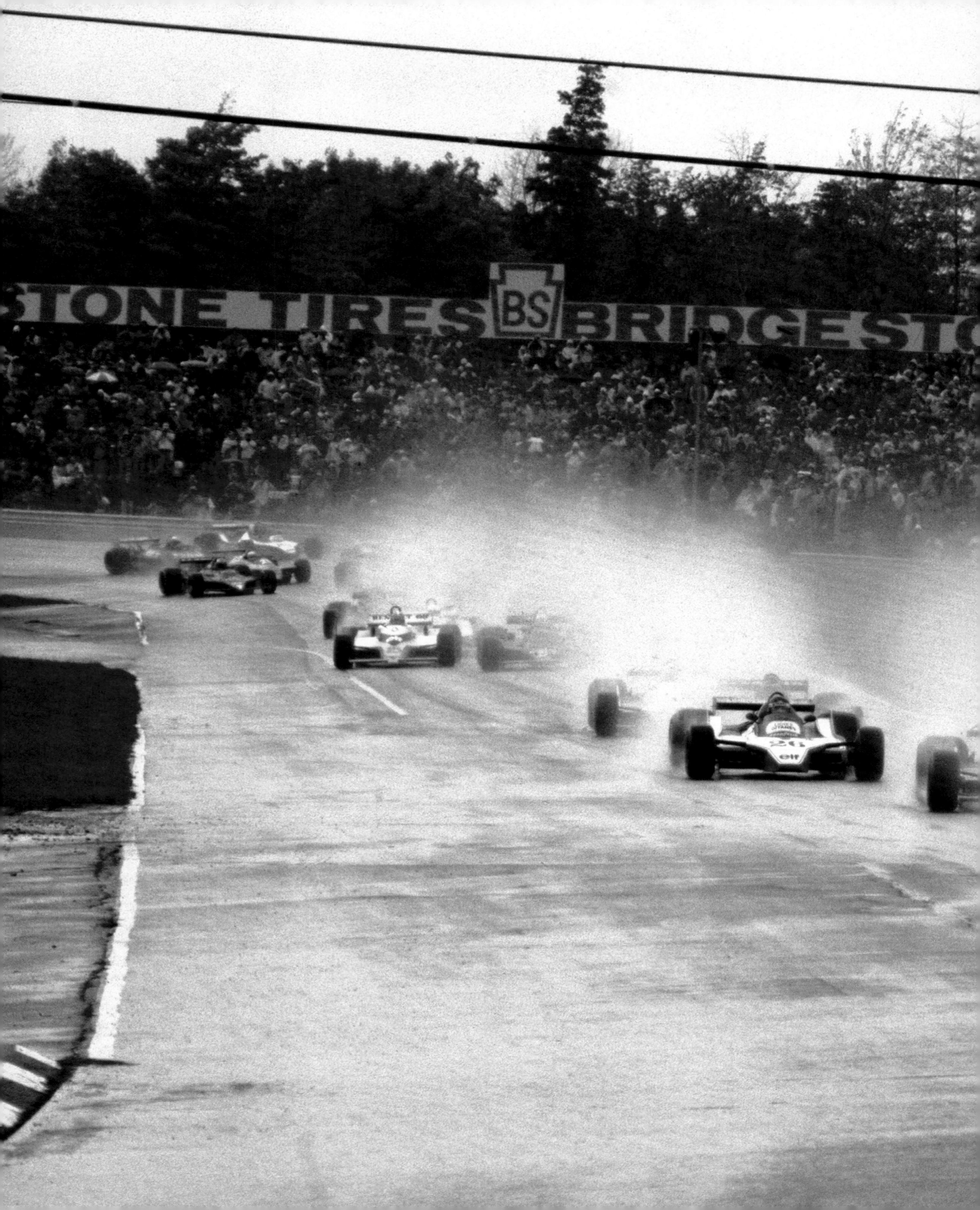
STONE TIRES
BS
BRIDGESTO

ABOVE The sliding skirts of the Ferrari T4 are functioning perfectly as Gilles revels in the wet weather at the Glen. As the rain turned to drizzle, and then ceased, Alan Jones looked set to challenge the red car, but a wheel fell off the Williams after a badly executed mid-race pitstop for slick tyres. Jacques Laffite spun away his chances on the third lap.

RIGHT Gilles concludes his 1979 season on the highest note at Watkins Glen. His third victory of the season, matching Jody Scheckter's tally, secured Ferrari's 1-2 in the Drivers' championship and left the Scuderia's winning lead in the Constructors' series at 38 points. Scheckter failed to finish at the Glen due to a burst tyre – the only mechanical failure of his entire racing season. Gilles's car had broken on four occasions – and, in this race, Gilles drove the last 40 laps nursing an engine with fading oil pressure.

1980

TRAPPED IN AN UNCOMPETITIVE CAR

Ferrari had concentrated its resources on a new turbo project, but had its 312T5 ready for the opening round of the 1980 championship – which signalled a sharp downturn in the team's performances. The T5 had greater wing area, thanks to a new, tapered monocoque, but the width of the 3-litre flat-12 still restricted air tunnel volume relative to the Cosworth V8 cars, on which ground-effect was now being exploited in earnest. The T5's handling was actually inferior to the T4's, in part because Michelin was now developing its tyres for the more powerful Renault V6 turbo. And now the Ferrari engine, even with new cylinder heads, was also down on power relative to the best DFVs... Thus equipped, Gilles and Jody Scheckter endured a dreadful season. Two fifth-place finishes and two sixths were all that Gilles could muster, and Scheckter, the defending world champion, fared even worse. Having scored a record 113 points in 1979, Ferrari amassed eight in 1980.

RIGHT Gilles hooks a thumb under a spoke of the steering wheel of his Ferrari 312T5 as he turns it through the Station hairpin at Monaco. Gilles's courage and car control yielded an unlikely sixth on the grid here, while Jody Scheckter, the winner the previous May, languished in 17th position, over a second slower.

ABOVE Gilles gets to meet the great Juan Manuel Fangio during a break in the action in Argentina. Perhaps he is just starting to run through the faults of the Ferrari T5.

RIGHT The new Ferrari was simply not competitive on the long straights and fast sweeps of the Buenos Aires circuit. Gilles could qualify only eighth, Jody Scheckter 11th as he began his title defence. On the opening lap, at the end of the back straight, Gilles had a high-speed trip across the grass that would have petrified a lesser mortal, but lurched back onto the tarmac in 12th position. Making the best use of the tight infield section that ended the 3.7-mile lap, he recovered eighth place by lap 5 and, after catching and repassing his team mate, fifth on lap 10. Aided by only two retirements, he was solidly established in second position on lap 30 – and crashed on lap 36. He noticed that the straight-ahead position of his steering wheel had altered as he sped down the back straight. When he turned the wheel entering the right-hander behind the pits, nothing happened. The car shot through catchfencing there and struck the barrier very hard, leaving Gilles wide-eyed but unscathed.

LEFT Gilles goes for a gap between the Renault of pole man Jean-Pierre Jabouille and Didier Pironi's Ligier-DFV at the start in Brazil.

ABOVE The Ferrari was in the lead as they arrived at the first turn at Interlagos. But it was swiftly in tyre trouble, and Gilles slipped back down the order before pitting for new rubber after only seven laps.

LEFT Gilles leads Jean-Pierre Jabouille's Renault, the Ligiers of Didier Pironi and Jacques Laffite and René Arnoux's winning Renault before his tyres went off at Interlagos. Rejoining the Brazilian Grand Prix in 20th place, driving with one eye on his tyres, he grimly raced back up to seventh. And then, with five laps remaining, a bolt worked loose and jammed the throttle mechanism. Gilles had to spin the T5 to stop it.

RIGHT There was no matching the turbocharged Renaults on the high-altitude Kyalami circuit near Johannesburg, and Gilles and Jody Scheckter could qualify only on the fifth row, 2sec and more away from the pace of the yellow cars. Both men then had blown engines. In the race, the Ferrari drivers again struggled with their Michelins. Gilles, here pursued by Alan Jones's Williams, spun off the track on the third lap and had to pit twice for fresh tyres. As he left pit lane the second time, the T5's transmission "broke"...

LEFT Ferrari conducted a lot of testing during the four weeks following the South African Grand Prix and came up with some modifications to the T5 for Long Beach, but they made little difference to the car's traction. Here Gilles takes his car beyond its limit in trying to improve on 10th position in qualifying. The next day, he was the star of the US Grand Prix West. He scythed through the field and emerged in third place shortly before halfway. After a dozen laps, closing on leaders Nelson Piquet and Alan Jones, he was clipped as he lapped Derek Daly's Tyrrell, and had to pit for a new nose section. The crew didn't fit it properly, and he had to stop again a lap after rejoining. His anger was again transmitted all the way through the powertrain to a driveshaft, which immediately succumbed.

LEFT Gilles and Joann in pit lane at Zolder, back in Europe for the Belgian Grand Prix. He qualified an unhappy 12th, directly ahead of Jody Scheckter, and finished sixth thanks mainly to attrition. He was lapped 20 laps before the finish by race winner Didier Pironi, but at least it was his first championship point of the season.

RIGHT Gilles avoided involvement in a first-corner accident at Monaco only by taking refuge in the Ste Devote escape road. Rejoining the track in a cloud of rubber smoke, yet again he spectacularly exceeded all expectations for the T5. He took no prisoners over the first 20 laps as, somehow, he forced a way back up to seventh place. A stop for new tyres had no effect on his determination and he finished fifth. Scheckter was long parked, having given up on the car's "impossible" handling.

LEFT Gilles's equipment in Monaco was a substantially revised T5 from the hard-pressed engineers of the Gestione Sportiva in Maranello. It had a 100mm shorter wheelbase and a smaller front wing, while the rear wing relocated ahead of the rear axle. The car still handled like a dog.

LEFT Gilles corners the T5 during the British Grand Prix at Brands Hatch, the scene of his dominant Race of Champions victory the previous year. Things were very different now. He was embarking on the second half of a wretched season. He went to England with only three finishes to his name, and championship points only for a sixth at Zolder and the hard-won fifth at Monaco. The red cars were now hopelessly off the pace and qualified 19th and 23rd, Gilles ahead. An engine failure ended his misery after 35 laps.

ABOVE LEFT A pit-lane conference with Mauro Forghieri at Hockenheim during practice for the German Grand Prix. Unlike some other Ferrari race drivers, Gilles swiftly established a rapport with the Scuderia's technical director. "I like him," Gilles said of Forghieri. "He's strong-headed, and doesn't give up trying to reach any objective. He's an exceptional man and I've learned a lot from him."

LEFT Gilles began to make serious money in 1979-80 when he attracted a number of personal sponsorship and endorsement deals. Some of his new-found wealth was spent on an apartment in Monaco, and some of the change on expensive 'toys' including several cars, a Jeep and a helicopter, which he now used to travel to European races. Here Joann (at left) heads for the paddock from the landing field on the Osterreichring.

ABOVE Scuderia Ferrari's need for new equipment was acute long before September 1980, when its all-new, V6 turbo powered 126C was seen in public for the first time at Imola, the scene that season of the Italian Grand Prix. Gilles drove the car on the Saturday morning there and was so encouraged that he set a qualifying time with it in the afternoon. He went over half a second quicker than his best with the recalcitrant T5, but the 126C was not yet race-ready. The team declined to press the new ground-effect car into service, and it was not used in anger until 1981.

LEFT Gilles reverted to the flat-12 Ferrari for the Italian Grand Prix and started strongly, storming up from eighth on the grid to fourth position inside the first four laps. On the sixth lap, his right rear tyre exploded as he sped through the 180mph kink before the Tosa corner. The T5 hurtled into the barrier, and Gilles was struck on the head by the left front wheel as the whole of that side of the car was ripped away. He escaped with a headache.

BELOW Inhabitants of Nerviano, a town near the Autodromo Nazionale di Monza, brought this message for Gilles on their day trip to the Autodromo Enzo e Dino Ferrari. The Italian fans already loved him as no other driver in Ferrari history..

ABOVE Oversteering the awful T5 out of the hairpin in Montréal. Gilles had won his home Grand Prix in 1978, and finished a close second in 1979. This time, he qualified 22nd – and Jody Scheckter was eight-tenths slower, thus failing to qualify for the first time in his career. But Gilles's progress on race day was exceptional even by his standards. He drove a fabulous race, and finished fifth.

RIGHT Signed to replace Jody Scheckter, who had retired, Didier Pironi shakes the hand of Enzo Ferrari after a media conference in Maranello announcing the Scuderia's team for 1981. Gilles and Joann look on. Gilles reckoned that meeting Ferrari was "like an audience with the Pope".

ABOVE Gilles left the dreadful T5 experience behind him at Watkins Glen by qualifying 18th for the US Grand Prix, and then deranging his suspension against a barrier on race day. Relieved that 1980 was done, he returned to Europe eager to continue testing the turbocharged 126C, here at Paul Ricard.

1 9 8 1

TWO GREAT VICTORIES WITH THE TURBO

Gilles and his new team mate, Didier Pironi, were the first Scuderia Ferrari drivers to race a turbocharged Formula 1 car as the team became the first to follow the trail blazed (often literally) by Renault over the previous four seasons. The 1.5-litre V6 in the new, ground-effect 126CK developed upwards of 545bhp, thus maintaining Ferrari's reputation for power, but throttle lag was a real problem. In addition, the car was not as well integrated as the best Cosworth opposition from Brabham and Williams, and substantially heavier. With development of the new engine a clear priority, the chassis had taken second place. At no point in the season did the handling come up to the drivers' expectations, and reliability was poor: Gilles was stopped on five occasions by mechanical failures. Despite all these shortcomings, he contrived to lead four of the 15 Grands Prix and to deliver two exceptional victories in mid-season, one of these with uncharacteristic finesse.

RIGHT Gilles was adept at overcoming the deficiencies of his car, but excelled himself in the 1981 Spanish Grand Prix. In place of the hard-charging, devil-may-care driver who had become so familiar, his rivals at Jarama found themselves trapped behind a Ferrari that was fast on the straights and impeccably driven through the turns.

ABOVE The 1981 season began in Long Beach, where Ferrari was still experimenting with two versions of the all-new, 120deg V6 engine, one with a Comprex supercharger and one with two KKK turbochargers (pictured). Gilles preferred the turbo but a holed piston meant he had to qualify with the supercharger – and a misfire. He qualified fifth on the grid, almost half a second quicker than his new team mate.

RIGHT Gilles and Didier Pironi were desperately disappointed in Long Beach with the handling of the Ferrari 126C. Both men were also hampered over the first two days of the race meeting by engine and gearbox failures.

ABOVE Gilles was joined in Long Beach by his brother, Jacques, who finished second in the Formula Atlantic support race, driving a March for Doug Shierson. Jacques had won the 1980 Canadian Atlantic title and would successfully defend it this season before arranging two end-of-year Formula 1 drives with Arrows. He failed to qualify in Montréal and Las Vegas. Jacques went on to win the Can-Am title in 1983 and, after again failing to put a RAM March on the Formula 1 grid that year in Montréal, to become the first Canadian to win a Champ Car race, at Elkhart Lake in 1985.

RIGHT For all their faults, the turbocharged Ferraris were the quickest in a straight line at Long Beach and Gilles shot into the lead of the US Grand Prix West as they raced along Shoreline Drive for the first time. His momentum took him past his braking point and he slid wide at the Queens hairpin. Riccardo Patrese in the pole position Arrows and the Williams drivers, Carlos Reutemann and Alan Jones, all went inside him, but he muscled his way back into the pack ahead of Nelson Piquet (Brabham), Eddie Cheever in the blue Tyrrell and Didier Pironi in the other Ferrari. A broken driveshaft halted him after 17 laps.

LEFT After failing to qualify on the front two rows at the first three 'flyaway' Grands Prix, and to finish any of them, Gilles startled everyone by putting his 126CK on pole position for the first European race, at Imola, seven-tenths quicker than Carlos Reutemann. This was the Scuderia's first pole since Monaco 1979. Lined up behind the Williams are René Arnoux and Alain Prost in the turbo Renaults, Nelson Piquet (Brabham), Didier Pironi in the other red car and John Watson (McLaren). Gilles led the first 14 laps on a drying track surface, in an unexpected 1-2 with Pironi, and then stopped for slicks – the first of the front-runners to do so. It began to rain as he left the pits. He had to return for another set of grooved tyres two laps later, and his race was ruined. Yet he produced a terrific drive to seventh place. Piquet won as Pironi, his tyres finished, faded to fifth.

ABOVE Gilles powers along the back straight at Zolder in his 'standard' 126CK. Didier Pironi's car was equipped for the Belgian Grand Prix with a hydraulic suspension system that delivered an immediate improvement in handling. Gilles qualified seventh, half a second slower than his team mate, but he had the better of it on race day.

RIGHT Gilles listens to Pironi, sitting on a sidepod of his team mate's car in third position on the overcrowded dummy grid at Zolder. Pironi led the race but fading brakes dropped him to eighth, while a consistent run by Gilles with an ill-handling car yielded fourth place.

LEFT Lap one of the 1981 Monaco Grand Prix, and Gilles points his Ferrari at the Tabac left-hander in pursuit of Nelson Piquet's race-leading Brabham. Following are Nigel Mansell (Lotus), Carlos Reutemann (Williams), Riccardo Patrese (Arrows), Elio de Angelis (Lotus), Alan Jones (Williams) and the next best non-Cosworth drivers, Jacques Laffite (Ligier-Matra V12) and Alain Prost (Renault turbo). A fine drive by Jones took him through the pack, past Gilles on the 20th lap, and up with Piquet on the 40th. Piquet cracked under the pressure and tripped himself up when lapping backmarkers.

ABOVE Gilles tucks closely into the barrier at the apex of the right-hander in Casino Square, running a strong second ahead of Mansell and Reutemann.

LEFT Gilles passes the abandoned Renault of René Arnoux during his winning drive in the Monaco Grand Prix. Renault had started the turbo revolution in 1977 (in Gilles's maiden race at Silverstone) and had won for the first time in 1979 (at Dijon, where only Gilles's bravado had prevented a French 1-2). That success had prompted Mauro Forghieri to press the button on Ferrari's own turbo project in the Gestione Sportiva. In the meantime, Renault had won three more races, and forced induction was now clearly the future.

LEFT Gilles corners at Monaco, showing the overhead camera the lines of the turbo V6 Ferrari that had been designed under the direction of Mauro Forghieri. He ceded pole position to Brabham's Nelson Piquet by less than a tenth of a second.

ABOVE Alan Jones took the lead at Monaco when Piquet crashed out on lap 54. Gilles's Ferrari was now in second place but half a minute behind, and its brakes were fading. The race seemed to be over. Then, with nine laps remaining, Jones felt his DFV 'hunting' and made a quick stop for fuel, rejoining only 6sec in front of Gilles. But his engine continued to splutter, and the Ferrari closed in relentlessly. Gilles caught the Williams here at the Station hairpin five laps from the finish, and passed it for good when they reached the start-finish straight.

LEFT An empty road behind him, Gilles cruises under the chequered flag to claim the first Grand Prix victory by a turbocharged Ferrari.

BELOW Sharing a private moment with Joann on the Monaco podium after his unexpected victory. He said afterwards: "It was one of the most tiring races of my life. The suspension was so stiff, it was like a go-kart, and now I ache all over. When the brakes started to go away, I had to be very brutal with my car, particularly the gearbox, but it lasted OK. I am very lucky today..."

LEFT Having won at Monaco with an ailing car, Gilles followed up with an equally remarkable victory in the next race, at Jarama, where he showed talents he had hidden hitherto – for extreme precision and discipline. In a way, it was his finest hour. When pole man Jacques Laffite bogged down at the start of the Spanish Grand Prix, Alan Jones took off into the lead, but the best start by far was made by Gilles. From seventh on the grid, he rocketed into third place behind Carlos Reutemann in the other Williams, and then grabbed second place in the first turn of the second lap. Jones spun off the track on the 14th lap, and now the Ferrari was leading. Just...

ABOVE The order behind Gilles changed from time to time: in this late-race shot, Laffite is in second place ahead of John Watson (McLaren), Reutemann and Elio de Angelis (Lotus). Gilles used the power of his turbo V6 to keep ahead of the pursuing cars on the straights, and very tight lines in the turns to thwart their superior handling. As a result, the race lap times were often 5sec and more slower than the pole position time. The leading group spent the final 20 laps or so like this, and it finished with these five covered by 1.24sec at the chequer.

RIGHT A rare photograph of Gilles actually oversteering his Ferrari at Jarama, establishing that it was, indeed, slippery off the racing line all round the Madrid circuit that day. The Ferrari V6 had the legs on everyone on the straights and could stop with the best of them (with an acceleration of 2.9g). As long as Gilles stayed on the line in the turns, no way would he be overtaken.

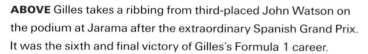

ABOVE Gilles takes a ribbing from third-placed John Watson on the podium at Jarama after the extraordinary Spanish Grand Prix. It was the sixth and final victory of Gilles's Formula 1 career.

RIGHT The Ferrari 126CK was an appalling handful at Dijon-Prénois for the French Grand Prix, porpoising wildly on the straights as well as misbehaving as usual in the turns. It came as no surprise during practice when Gilles buried his car in the catchfencing. As it happened, he was wired at the time for a medical experiment. The read-outs showed that his heart rate in his bucking bronco never exceeded 127 during the laps prior to this 130mph shunt, and spiked to only 168 during the accident itself. The winner of the previous two races took the spare car and qualified 11th, half a second quicker than his team mate (registering a heart rate of 182 in the process). On race day, he hauled himself as high as sixth before he was halted by an electrical failure.

LEFT Turbocharging came to the fore at Silverstone, where the Renaults monopolised the front row and Didier Pironi qualified fourth for Ferrari, although the Italian cars were no match for the French except on the straights. Gilles, here pressed into conversation by his team mate, struggled with his engine and lined up in eighth position.

ABOVE Gilles produced another meteoric getaway in the British Grand Prix. For him, the red lights used at the time didn't turn to green, because he was blind to that colour. They just went out... This is the opening lap. Leader Alain Prost is out of shot as Pironi and Villeneuve lead René Arnoux. The Renault was soon past both of them and pursuing its sister car.

LEFT On the fourth lap at Silverstone, Gilles clipped a kerb in the Woodcote chicane and his Ferrari went light, coming down on its rock-hard suspension and bouncing out of his control. It careened into the catchfencing there, taking with it Alan Jones's Williams and the McLaren of an unsighted Andrea de Cesaris. Gilles extracted what was left of his car and headed, Zandvoort-style, towards the pits.

ABOVE The damaged Ferrari 126CK lasted only as far as Stowe corner after its mauling in the Woodcote catchfences.

LEFT This was his fourth full season as a Formula 1 driver, but Gilles never did stop trying to find the limits of his racecars. This heart-stopping moment occurred during qualifying on the Osterreichring, as he got on the brakes at the top of the steep start-finish straight before the Hella Licht S-bend. Alan Jones is the spectator.

ABOVE Gilles is strapped into his Ferrari after qualifying third on the Osterreichring, behind only the Renaults.

RIGHT He made another great start in the Austrian Grand Prix, squeezing between René Arnoux and the pit wall, and emerging in the lead before they reached Hella Licht. Behind Alain Prost and alongside Arnoux is Jacques Laffite (Ligier), while Williams drivers Carlos Reutemann and Alan Jones are split by Nelson Piquet (Brabham) and Didier Pironi in the other Ferrari. The second time through Hella Licht, Gilles missed his braking point, damaged his skirts in the run-off area, rejoined – and crashed out of the race on the 12th lap at the Boschkurve. Before the race was finished, he was in his helicopter, hovering over the circuit for a while, using it make a bow to the main grandstand, then heading for home.

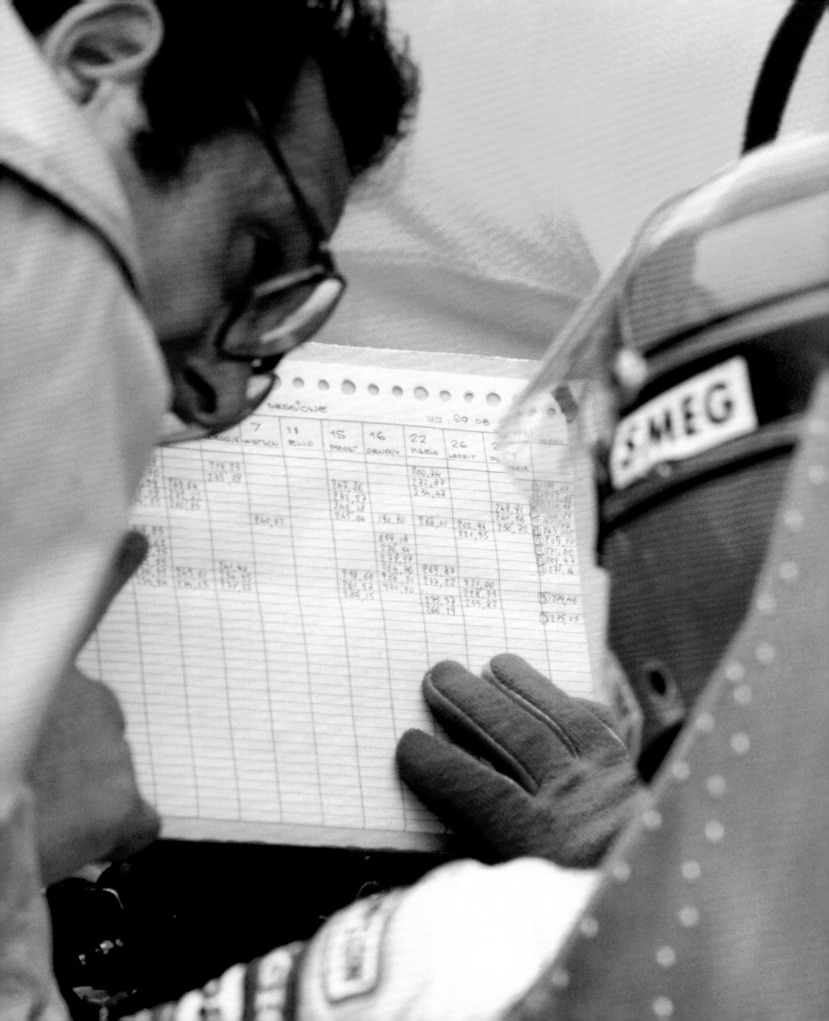

LEFT Gilles tells Mauro Forghieri why he could only qualify 16th for the Dutch Grand Prix, and his team mate 12th. The 126CK was still difficult to control, largely due to its ultra-hard suspension setup. Not only that, but its only forte – its tremendous pace in a straight line – had somehow gone missing at this race.

ABOVE Come race day at Zandvoort, Gilles made an impact – but only with the barrier at the first corner. From the eighth row of the grid, yet another fast start was his undoing, because he was punted off the track when Bruno Giacomelli's Alfa Romeo veered into his path.

NEXT PAGE Scuderia Ferrari in pit lane at Zandvoort. Gilles awaits his bodywork as Didier Pironi is strapped into his cockpit.

LEFT Ferrari brought four cars to Monza but it didn't help Gilles. Didier Pironi crashed heavily during the first qualifying session, then blew an engine early in the second session, and was switched to Gilles's spare. When Gilles also lost an engine, he had nothing to qualify. Here he climbs aboard his car in pit lane before taking his ninth spot on the starting grid. He was in sixth place after only three laps, but then his turbocharger broke.

RIGHT Making a point to Didier Pironi in Montréal. Their Ferraris handling worse than ever, they shared the sixth row of the starting grid for the Canadian Grand Prix. Both men had incidents and Gilles calmly explained: "The car has no suspension movement. It jumps six or seven feet to the left when it goes over the bumps entering the corner after the pits."

ABOVE Joy for Gilles! Race day in Montréal, and it's raining. Emerging as the winner of a chicken run on the first lap with Didier Pironi and René Arnoux, which sent his team mate spinning and the Renault into the wall, Gilles fought the 126CK from 11th place to third after just seven laps. He passed Alain Prost's Renault on the 15th lap to take second place behind Jacques Laffite. But his engine developed a water-induced misfire, and he could mount no challenge to the Ligier-Matra.

ABOVE RIGHT Gilles savaged the front wing of his Ferrari when lapping Elio de Angelis's Lotus during his fine drive in Canada. The dislodged wing then obstructed his view until it finally broke off completely. He was passed by John Watson's McLaren but, balancing his car at lurid angles in the absence of front downforce, cheered the sodden spectators by finishing a fighting third.

RIGHT Back on the podium at last, Gilles celebrates third place in his home Grand Prix with winner Laffite (centre) and Watson.

LEFT At high altitude in Las Vegas, Gilles was able to qualify third. Pole man Carlos Reutemann made a poor start and Gilles grabbed second place before the first corner behind Alan Jones in the other Williams, forcing Alain Prost's Renault out wide. Gilles was halted by another turbo failure when he was on the point of being disqualified, anyway, for lining up his car outside his box. It seemed an appropriate way to end a season with only two highlights, bright though they had been.

1982

A CHAMPIONSHIP BID CUT SHORT

For 1982, Ferrari produced a more effective chassis, the 126C2, with which Gilles and Didier Pironi could oppose the Renaults, the best Cosworth cars and the Brabham-BMW turbos that were under development. By now, the science of ground-effect had spawned a generation of brutal racecars with awesome – and clearly dangerous – cornering performance. With their skirts glued to the track surface and zero suspension movement, they were powerful, unforgiving and immensely heavy to drive. The drivers hated them, Gilles included. After the second race in Brazil, he said: "The g-forces are unbelievable. If you go over a bump as you turn into a corner, you lose vision. Everything goes blurred. The g-forces will be less at Imola. But Zolder, I guess, will be quite a good killer..." At Imola, his win was stolen when he was blatantly double-crossed by his team mate. At Zolder, he went for a banzai qualifying lap, trying to beat Pironi's time, and it ended in unspeakable horror.

RIGHT At three-quarter distance in the San Marino Grand Prix at Imola, Gilles and Didier Pironi found themselves holding a comfortable 1-2. The Ferrari pit showed them a 'slow' board (an instruction to hold station). But Pironi famously defied team orders and overtook Gilles on the very last lap.

LEFT Signing autographs during the opening race meeting of the 1982 season, at Kyalami. The new Ferrari 126C2, a big improvement on the 1981 car with a stiffer, bonded and riveted aluminium chassis designed by Harvey Postlethwaite, had done very promising lap times in pre-season testing at Fiorano. Gilles's hopes were high. He qualified a brand new chassis third for the South African Grand Prix. René Arnoux drove a scintillating pole for Renault, but Gilles was right among the new, turbocharged Brabhams of Nelson Piquet and Riccardo Patrese and Alain Prost's fifth-placed Renault.

ABOVE Gilles's optimism was brief. On race day, he established his Ferrari in third place behind the fast-starting Renaults, but he was stopped by a broken turbocharger on only the seventh lap.

LEFT First practice on the Jacarepagua circuit near Rio de Janeiro with the Ferrari 126C2. Gilles, wearing a neck brace here for the first time to cope with g-forces, produced a tremendous lap-time, but was pipped for pole by Alain Prost's Renault. Halfway round the lap, he had a close call when he very nearly clipped a slow-moving car. "Making space," he called his reaction, and thought no more of the incident. Didier Pironi was nursing a sore leg after destroying Gilles's Kyalami chassis when its throttle jammed open in testing at Paul Ricard. He qualified eighth.

ABOVE Prost made a poor start in the Brazilian Grand Prix and Gilles was quick to take the lead, hounded by Nelson Piquet for Brabham and Carlos Reutemann for Williams. On the 30th lap, Piquet forced Gilles wide and he put two wheels on the dirt, and crashed out. Piquet went on to win his home race.

LEFT At Long Beach in the Ferrari 126C2, now with front aerofoils. Mauro Forghieri devised an ingenious but ill-advised aerodynamic solution for this third round of the championship. The rules stated that no item of 'coachwork' behind the rear wheels (the wing) could be more than 110cm wide, but Forghieri noticed that they didn't say how many such items were allowed. So he fitted two aerofoils, each 110cm wide, effectively giving Gilles and Didier Pironi full-width rear wings.

ABOVE Gilles finished third in the US Grand Prix West, which brought new McLaren signing Niki Lauda (left) his first win since returning to Formula 1 after two seasons away. But Forghieri, the engineer he admired so much, let Gilles down on this occasion. Those wings were protested and he was disqualified.

RIGHT The San Marino Grand Prix was boycotted by the Formula One Constructors Association, in futile protest against the disqualifications of the Brabham and Williams that had finished first and second in Brazil. The FOCA teams had been in the carefree habit of topping up with water after the races to bring their cars up to the minimum weight before post-race scrutineering. The factory teams of Alfa Romeo, Ferrari and Renault were joined at Imola by ATS, Osella, Toleman and Tyrrell, the last-named the only FOCA member to break ranks. Here a diminished group of 13 Formula 1 drivers assembles for the pre-race briefing. Among them are Alain Prost, Andrea de Cesaris, Manfred Winkelhock and Bruno Giacomelli (all facing Gilles) and, behind him, Didier Pironi, Jean-Pierre Jarier, Eliseo Salazar and Teo Fabi, with Ricardo Paletti, Michele Alboreto, Brian Henton and Derek Warwick beyond. They appear to be waiting for René Arnoux.

BELOW Gilles qualified third at Imola behind the Renaults, Pironi fourth after a big accident when a tyre went down.

LEFT The Imola crowd didn't care that there were only 14 cars – as long as two of them were Ferraris, they didn't see any problem. René Arnoux's Renault did most of the leading over the first 44 of 60 laps, but the red cars had the yellow one under constant pressure. On lap 45, the Renault blew its engine and, to the unbridled joy of the spectators, caught fire as Arnoux parked it. Now Gilles led Pironi in red formation, miles ahead of the rest. They were shown the 'slow' board.

ABOVE Pironi-Villeneuve: that was how it was as the chequered flag fell. Pironi had passed Gilles on lap 53 and chopped across him a couple of times when he tried to repass. Their lap times tumbled but, when Gilles got back in front on the penultimate lap, onlookers were satisfied that it had all been for show. It hadn't. Pironi took Gilles unawares as they began the final lap and drafted past him at 180mph on the run down to Tosa, and held on to win by three-tenths of a second.

LEFT Gilles joins Pironi on the Imola podium, but his emotions are clear for all to see. "He looked like the hero who had won the race, and I looked like the spoiled bastard who sulked," said Gilles bitterly of this scene.

ABOVE Jackie Stewart tries to engage Gilles after the podium ceremonies, but he is quite inconsolable. He said later: "It was going to be my race because I was in front of Pironi when Arnoux dropped out. We got a 'slow' signal, and that means 'hold station'. It's not true there are no team orders at Ferrari. If it had been the other way round, well, tough luck for me. I wouldn't have tried to take the lead away from him. Jesus, we've been living together at Ferrari for a year and a half. I thought I knew the guy. I trusted him." He never uttered another word to Pironi. He referred to him simply as: "The thief."

LEFT Two weeks after Imola, with the entire Formula 1 field reassembled for the Belgian Grand Prix, Gilles began his Zolder weekend on the Friday by lapping 1.3sec faster than Didier Pironi in the first qualifying session, when his detested team mate was hampered by an electrical fault. Here, the following day, Gilles is wired through to race engineer Antonio Tomaini in pit lane.

RIGHT Mauro Forghieri (at right) hurries to say something to Gilles just before the start of the fateful final qualifying session.

NEXT PAGE Each driver was restricted to two sets of qualifying tyres in each session. On his first set of soft tyres on the Saturday, Gilles set a lap time that would have put him seventh on the grid for the Belgian Grand Prix. But then Pironi went a tenth quicker. Gilles waited until 10 minutes before the end of the session before leaving the pits on his final set of qualifying tyres.

LEFT An appalling scene at the Terlamenbocht corner. Eight minutes before the end of the final qualifying session, Gilles crested a brow between the chicane and this right-hand turn, and would have caught his first glimpse of Jochen Mass's March, which was on its in-lap and cruising. Mass was alert and saw the Ferrari in his mirrors. He moved right to give it room to pass on the inside of a flat-out, 150mph, left-hand sweep known as Sacramentshelling that led into the Terlamenbocht. In the same split-second, Gilles committed himself to the outside. The Ferrari's left front wheel clipped the March's right rear, and the red car hurtled to destruction. The front of the C2 was ripped away and Gilles was hurled out of the chassis, still strapped into his seat. He received multiple injuries, including a broken neck, and died in hospital during the evening.

ABOVE The remains of Gilles's Ferrari are craned onto a low-loader at the scene of an accident that shocked and dismayed all Formula 1 fans, and broke the heart of many. Jochen Mass was completely exonerated by a subsequent FIA inquiry, which blamed: "Driver error on the part of Gilles Villeneuve."

LEFT A sombre moment in Montréal immediately after the 1982 Canadian Grand Prix, five weeks after the tragedy at Zolder. The track on the Ile de Notre Dame, in the St Lawrence river, had been renamed for Gilles, and his father, Séville Villeneuve, is on the podium, holding the trophy. The first three finishers, Nelson Piquet, Riccardo Patrese and John Watson, are all visibly subdued. They are thinking not only of Gilles, but also of Ricardo Paletti. Making his first start in Formula 1, from the back of the grid, Paletti had been killed in a 120mph impact when his Osella collided with Didier Pironi's Ferrari, which had stalled in pole position.

LEFT The memorial to Gilles at the Zolder circuit. For many thousands of his fans, the light was extinguished from motor racing on the day he died. The town of Berthierville was jammed with mourners, including Canadian prime minister Pierre Trudeau, when his funeral was held in the 200-year-old church there. A bronze bust was made of him for the entrance to Ferrari's test track at Fiorano, a Canadian flag was painted on the tarmac at Imola at the spot from which he started his last race, and a museum was dedicated to his memory in Berthierville, his home town.

RIGHT In action again: the Ferrari 312T3 with which Gilles achieved his maiden Formula 1 victory, in the 1978 Canadian Grand Prix. His son, Jacques, is in the cockpit during the 2004 Goodwood Festival of Speed, wearing one of his father's helmets.

RIGHT Jacques Villeneuve was 11 years old when his father was killed, but motor racing was in his blood. He would have made his father proud. Determined to make it to Formula 1 through his own endeavours, and not his surname, Jacques achieved his ambition after successes in Italy and Japan in Formula 3, and in North America in Toyota Atlantic and Champ Car racing, winning the 1995 Indianapolis 500 and the title. In his début season in F1 with Williams in 1996, four wins took him to second place in the championship behind team mate Damon Hill. Seven more victories delivered the 1997 title. He moved to BAR in 1999 and his career began to peter out. After three outings for Renault in 2004, he was signed by Sauber but was replaced after the 2006 German Grand Prix. Jacques's F1 career tally was 11 wins from 165 races, Gilles's six from 67. The latter's is a better strike rate – but Gilles never won the title. His genes did...

RACE RESULTS

Compiled by David Hayhoe

1973

Québec Provincial Formula Ford Championship — won 7 of 10 events

1974

Date	Country/event	Circuit	Race no.	Car	Model	Engine	Configuration	Notes	Grid position	Result
26/05	Player's Formula Atlantic	Westwood		March	74B	Ford Cosworth	4			3
02/06	Player's Formula Atlantic	Edmonton		March	74B	Ford Cosworth	4		6	22
16/06	Player's Formula Atlantic	Gimli		March	74B	Ford Cosworth	4	engine	15	r
01/07	Player's Formula Atlantic	Mosport Park	13	March	74B	Ford Cosworth	4	accident/injury	14	r
11/08	Player's Formula Atlantic	Halifax		March	74B	Ford Cosworth	4	gave up		r
01/09	Molson Grand Prix (F Atlantic)	Trios-Rivières		March	74B	Ford Cosworth	4	accident	13	r

1975

Date	Country/event	Circuit	Race no.	Car	Model	Engine	Configuration	Notes	Grid position	Result
25/05	Player's Formula Atlantic	Edmonton		March	75B	Ford Cosworth	4			15
01/06	Player's Formula Atlantic	Westwood		March	75B	Ford Cosworth	4		8	5
22/06	Player's Formula Atlantic	Gimli		March	75B	Ford Cosworth	4		19	1
06/07	Player's Formula Atlantic	St. Jovite		March	75B	Ford Cosworth	4	fastest lap	4	2
20/07	Player's Formula Atlantic	Mosport Park		March	75B	Ford Cosworth	4			17
17/08	Player's Formula Atlantic	Halifax		March	75B	Ford Cosworth	4		7	14
31/08	Molson Grand Prix (F Atlantic)	Trios-Rivières	69	March	75B	Ford Cosworth	4	brakes	3	r
07/09	Formula Atlantic	Donnybrooke		March	75B	Ford Cosworth	4			4

1976

Date	Country/event	Circuit	Race no.	Car	Model	Engine	Configuration	Notes	Grid position	Result
31/01	Daytona 24 Hours (IMSA GT)	Daytona		Chevrolet	Camaro	Chevrolet	V8	(with Mo Carter) engine	8	r
11/04	IMSA Formula Atlantic	Road Atlanta		March	76B	Ford Cosworth	4		1	1
02/05	IMSA Formula Atlantic	Laguna Seca		March	76B	Ford Cosworth	4			1
09/05	IMSA Formula Atlantic	Ontario		March	76B	Ford Cosworth	4	fastest lap	1	1
16/05	Player's Formula Atlantic	Edmonton		March	76B	Ford Cosworth	4	fastest lap	1	1
30/05	Player's Formula Atlantic	Westwood		March	76B	Ford Cosworth	4	engine/accident	1	r
07/06	Pau Grand Prix (Euro F2)	Pau		March	762	Hart	4	overheating	10	r
13/06	Player's Formula Atlantic	Gimli		March	76B	Ford Cosworth	4		1	1
11/07	Player's Formula Atlantic	St. Jovite		March	76B	Ford Cosworth	4	fastest lap	1	1
08/08	Player's Formula Atlantic	Halifax		March	76B	Ford Cosworth	4	fastest lap	1	1
05/09	Molson Grand Prix (F Atlantic)	Trios-Rivières	69	March	76B	Ford Coworth	4	fastest lap	1	1
19/09	IMSA Formula Atlantic	Road Atlanta		March	76B	Ford Cosworth	4	fastest lap	1	1

1977

Date	Country/event	Circuit	Race no.	Car	Model	Engine	Configuration	Notes	Grid position	Result
15/01	Philips Formula Atlantic	Roy Hesketh		Chevron	B39	Ford Cosworth	4		10	3
29/01	Philips Formula Atlantic	Kyalami		Chevron	B39	Ford Cosworth	4		2	5
05/02	Philips Formula Atlantic	Goldfields		Chevron	B39	Ford Cosworth	4	mechanical	5	r
19/02	Philips Formula Atlantic	Killarney		Chevron	B39	Ford Cosworth	4	accident	5	r
22/05	Labatt's Formula Atlantic	Mosport Park		March	77B	Ford Cosworth	4	fastest lap	1	2
26/06	Labatt's Formula Atlantic	Gimli		March	77B	Ford Cosworth	4	engine	2	r
03/07	Labatt's Formula Atlantic	Edmonton		March	77B	Ford Cosworth	4		1	1
10/07	Can-Am	Watkins Glen	2	Wolf Dallara	WD1	Chevrolet	V8	gear linkage	4	r
16/07	BRITAIN	Silverstone	40	McLaren	M23	Ford Cosworth	V8		9	11
24/07	Can-Am	Elkhart Lake	2	Wolf Dallara	WD1	Chevrolet	V8		1	3
07/08	Labatt's Formula Atlantic	Halifax		March	77B	Ford Cosworth	4	accident	1	r
14/08	Labatt's Formula Atlantic	St. Félicien		March	77B	Ford Cosworth	4		1	1
20/08	Molson Diamond 6 Hours	Mosport Park		BMW	320i	BMW	6	with Eddie Cheever	11	3
21/08	Can-Am	Mosport Park	2	Wolf Dallara	WD1	Chevrolet	V8	wheel	6	r
04/09	Can-Am	Trois-Rivières	2	Wolf Dallara	WD1	Chevrolet	V8	gear linkage	3	r
04/09	Molson Grand Prix (F Atlantic)	Trois-Rivières	69	March	77B	Ford Cosworth	4		1	4
25/09	Labatt's Formula Atlantic	Québec City		March	77B	Ford Cosworth	4		3	1
09/10	CANADA	Mosport Park	21	Ferrari	312T2	Ferrari	F12	driveshaft	17	12r
23/10	JAPAN	Fuji	11	Ferrari	312T2	Ferrari	F12	accident	20	r

Date	Country/event	Circuit	Race no.	Car	Model	Engine	Configuration	Notes	Grid position	Result
15/01	ARGENTINA	Buenos Aires No.15	12	Ferrari	312T2	Ferrari	F12	fastest lap	7	8
29/01	BRAZIL	Rio de Janeiro	12	Ferrari	312T2	Ferrari	F12	accident	6	r
04/03	SOUTH AFRICA	Kyalami	12	Ferrari	312T3	Ferrari	F12	oil leak	8	r
02/04	USA WEST	Long Beach	12	Ferrari	312T3	Ferrari	F12	accident	2	r
07/05	MONACO	Monte Carlo	12	Ferrari	312T3	Ferrari	F12	front tyre burst/accident	8	r
21/05	BELGIUM	Zolder	12	Ferrari	312T3	Ferrari	F12		4	4
04/06	SPAIN	Jarama	12	Ferrari	312T3	Ferrari	F12		5	10
17/06	SWEDEN	Anderstorp	12	Ferrari	312T3	Ferrari	F12		7	9
02/07	FRANCE	Paul Ricard	12	Ferrari	312T3	Ferrari	F12		9	12
16/07	BRITAIN	Brands Hatch	12	Ferrari	312T3	Ferrari	F12	driveshaft	13	r
30/07	GERMANY	Hockenheim	12	Ferrari	312T3	Ferrari	F12		15	8
13/08	AUSTRIA	Österreichring	12	Ferrari	312T3	Ferrari	F12		11	3
27/08	NETHERLANDS	Zandvoort	12	Ferrari	312T3	Ferrari	F12		5	6
10/09	ITALY	Monza	12	Ferrari	312T3	Ferrari	F12		2	7
01/10	USA EAST	Watkins Glen	12	Ferrari	312T3	Ferrari	F12	engine	4	r
08/10	CANADA	Montréal	12	Ferrari	312T3	Ferrari	F12		3	1

Date	Country/event	Circuit	Race no.	Car	Model	Engine	Configuration	Notes	Grid position	Result
21/01	ARGENTINA	Buenos Aires No.15	12	Ferrari	312T3	Ferrari	F12	engine	10	12r
04/02	BRAZIL	Interlagos	12	Ferrari	312T3	Ferrari	F12		5	5
03/03	SOUTH AFRICA	Kyalami	12	Ferrari	312T4	Ferrari	F12	fastest lap	3	1
08/04	USA WEST	Long Beach	12	Ferrari	312T4	Ferrari	F12	fastest lap	1	1
15/04	Race of Champions	Brands Hatch	12	Ferrari	312T3	Ferrari	F12		3	1
29/04	SPAIN	Jarama	12	Ferrari	312T4	Ferrari	F12	fastest lap	3	7
13/05	BELGIUM	Zolder	12	Ferrari	312T4	Ferrari	F12	fastest lap/out of fuel	6	7r
27/05	MONACO	Monte Carlo	12	Ferrari	312T4	Ferrari	F12	transmission	2	r
01/07	FRANCE	Dijon Prenois	12	Ferrari	312T4	Ferrari	F12		3	2
14/07	BRITAIN	Silverstone	12	Ferrari	312T4	Ferrari	F12	fuel vaporisation	13	14r
29/07	GERMANY	Hockenheim	12	Ferrari	312T4	Ferrari	F12	fastest lap	9	8
12/08	AUSTRIA	Österreichring	12	Ferrari	312T4	Ferrari	F12		5	2
26/08	NETHERLANDS	Zandvoort	12	Ferrari	312T4	Ferrari	F12	fastest lap/suspension	6	r
09/09	ITALY	Monza	12	Ferrari	312T4	Ferrari	F12		5	2
16/09	Gran Premio Dino Ferrari	Imola	12	Ferrari	312T4B	Ferrari	F12	fastest lap	1	7
20-25/10	Giro d'Italia			Lancia Beta	M/Carlo	Lancia		with Röhrl/Geistdörfer		dq
30/09	CANADA	Montréal	12	Ferrari	312T4	Ferrari	F12		2	2
07/10	USA EAST	Watkins Glen	12	Ferrari	312T4	Ferrari	F12		3	1

Date	Country/event	Circuit	Race no.	Car	Model	Engine	Configuration	Notes	Grid position	Result
13/01	ARGENTINA	Buenos Aires No.15	2	Ferrari	312T5	Ferrari	F12	steering/accident	8	r
27/01	BRAZIL	Interlagos	2	Ferrari	312T5	Ferrari	F12	throttle jammed/spin	3	16r
01/03	SOUTH AFRICA	Kyalami	2	Ferrari	312T5	Ferrari	F12	transmission	10	r
30/03	USA WEST	Long Beach	2	Ferrari	312T5	Ferrari	F12	driveshaft	10	r
04/05	BELGIUM	Zolder	2	Ferrari	312T5	Ferrari	F12		12	6
18/05	MONACO	Monte Carlo	2	Ferrari	312T5	Ferrari	F12		6	5
29/06	FRANCE	Paul Ricard	2	Ferrari	312T5	Ferrari	F12		17	8
13/07	BRITAIN	Brands Hatch	2	Ferrari	312T5	Ferrari	F12	engine	19	r
10/08	GERMANY	Hockenheim	2	Ferrari	312T5	Ferrari	F12		16	6
17/08	AUSTRIA	Österreichring	2	Ferrari	312T5	Ferrari	F12		15	8
31/08	NETHERLANDS	Zandvoort	2	Ferrari	312T5	Ferrari	F12		7	7
14/09	ITALY	Imola	2	Ferrari	312T5	Ferrari	F12	rear tyre/accident	8	r
28/09	CANADA	Montréal	2	Ferrari	312T5	Ferrari	F12		22	5
05/10	USA EAST	Watkins Glen	2	Ferrari	312T5	Ferrari	F12	accident	18	r

Date	Country/event	Circuit	Race no.	Car	Model	Engine	Configuration	Notes	Grid position	Result
15/03	USA WEST	Long Beach	27	Ferrari	126CK	Ferrari	V6t	driveshaft	5	r
29/03	BRAZIL	Rio de Janeiro	27	Ferrari	126CK	Ferrari	V6t	turbo wastegate	7	r
12/04	ARGENTINA	Buenos Aires No.15	27	Ferrari	126CK	Ferrari	V6t	driveshaft	7	r
03/05	SAN MARINO	Imola	27	Ferrari	126CK	Ferrari	V6t	fastest lap	1	7
17/05	BELGIUM	Zolder	27	Ferrari	126CK	Ferrari	V6t		7	4
31/05	MONACO	Monte Carlo	27	Ferrari	126CK	Ferrari	V6t		2	1
21/06	SPAIN	Jarama	27	Ferrari	126CK	Ferrari	V6t		7	1
05/07	FRANCE	Dijon Prenois	27	Ferrari	126CK	Ferrari	V6t	electrics	11	r
18/07	BRITAIN	Silverstone	27	Ferrari	126CK	Ferrari	V6t	accident	8	r
02/08	GERMANY	Hockenheim	27	Ferrari	126CK	Ferrari	V6t		8	10
16/08	AUSTRIA	Österreichring	27	Ferrari	126CK	Ferrari	V6t	accident	3	r
30/08	NETHERLANDS	Zandvoort	27	Ferrari	126CK	Ferrari	V6t	accident	16	r
13/09	ITALY	Monza	27	Ferrari	126CK	Ferrari	V6t	turbo	9	r
27/09	CANADA	Montréal	27	Ferrari	126CK	Ferrari	V6t		11	3
17/10	CAESARS PALACE	Las Vegas	27	Ferrari	126CK	Ferrari	V6t	wrong grid position	3	dq

Date	Country/event	Circuit	Race no.	Car	Model	Engine	Configuration	Notes	Grid position	Result
23/01	SOUTH AFRICA	Kyalami	27	Ferrari	126C2	Ferrari	V6t	turbo	3	r
21/03	BRAZIL	Rio de Janeiro	27	Ferrari	126C2	Ferrari	V6t	accident	2	r
04/04	USA WEST	Long Beach	27	Ferrari	126C2	Ferrari	V6t	irregular wing	7	dq
25/04	SAN MARINO	Imola	27	Ferrari	126C2	Ferrari	V6t		3	2
09/05	BELGIUM	Zolder	27	Ferrari	126C2	Ferrari	V6t	fatal accident in qualifying		ns

My past is scarred with grief. I look back and I see my loved ones. And among my loved ones I see the face of **this great man: Gilles Villeneuve.**

ENZO FERRARI

He will remain as a member of the family of the truly great drivers in auto racing history. Gilles Villeneuve did not race to finish. He did not race for points. **He raced to win.** He was small in stature, but **he was a giant.**

JUAN MANUEL FANGIO

He was superb. His natural talent was phenomenal. There was **real genius in his car control.**

JACKIE STEWART

He was different from the rest of us. No human being can do miracles, you know, but Gilles made you wonder. **He was on a separate level.**

JACQUES LAFFITE

Gilles Villeneuve was **the fastest racing driver history has ever known.** He went doing something he loved. But he has not really gone. The memory of what he achieved will always be there.

JODY SCHECKTER

Gilles was **the perfect racing driver**. He was the craziest devil I ever came across. For all this, he was a sensitive and lovable character – **a unique human being.**

NIKI LAUDA

Gilles was **the last great driver.** The rest of us are just a bunch of good professionals.

ALAIN PROST